PLUSPLUS

PATTERNS FOR BETTER COMMUNICATION
FLORIAN MUECK

For permission requests, write to the publisher, at:
plusplus@florianmueck.com

www.florianmueck.com

Cover artwork, illustration & composing by www.navarra-design.com

Printed in the United States of America

ISBN 978-1-48180-361-8

Only dead fish swim with the flow.

ACKNOWLEDGMENTS

PLUSPLUS is not only a book. It's also an attitude. With their positive and constructive attitude, the people below continuously help me climb closer to that unreachable peak of the mountain of public speaking.

Special thanks to all my awesome clients.

Special thanks once again to Arthur Waters for his brilliance and patience on the editing side.

Special thanks to Conor Neill and IESE Business School — both are role models of personal and professional growth.

Special thanks to my Rhetoric-game partner and friend John Zimmer.

Special thanks to Olivia Schofield and her Spectacular Speakers for her neverending inspiration.

Special thanks to Michael Kalkowski for his priceless trust from the very beginning.

And, of course, very special thanks to my very special Rose.

For Prestigious Speakers

TABLE OF CONTENTS

II. DELIVERY

III. SLIDES   148

SLIDE BOOSTERS   149

SLIDE BRAKES   169

PLUSPLUS IS MAGIC!   179

THE PLUSPLUS PATTERN LIST   180

ABOUT THE AUTHOR   184

THE
MAGIC
OF
PLUSPLUS

Her name is Sonia, and she's from Mexico City. When I met her, I was about to give a seminar for the Foundation of Emotional Education[1] in Barcelona. Everyone was chatting and chaffering over their coffee before the training started — except Sonia, who was sitting alone at a table, hunched forward, poring over some notes.

I went over to her table and sat down. Instead of introducing myself, I just looked at her. Then I said: *You don't talk very much, do you?*

She answered: *No.*

Sonia was an introverted, timid, pensive person when I met her. She was insecure, reluctant to share even her ideas, much less her feelings, or her passions. It was as if she'd built a wall around herself, and was hiding behind it from everyone.

Two days later she had changed completely. Enthusiasm possessed her when she expressed her passion for archaeological museums. She modulated her voice to outstanding effect. She was poised; her self-confidence had soared. Now she positively radiated charisma. It was like magic.

What had happened to Sonia?

I lead seminars on public speaking. That is my profession. I've worked all across Europe, usually for major corporations. I've listened to and evaluated thousands of speeches — in three languages — and these thousands of evaluations have taught me one thing: the power of *feedback!*

I use only positive, constructive feedback: that is the secret magic of PLUSPLUS.

---

1   www.femeducacioemocional.org

PLUS: Sonia, what I liked in your speech was....

PLUSPLUS: Sonia, what you could have done even better was....

Who likes negative feedback? Who accepts MINUS feedback?

In my seminars, MINUS feedback is not allowed.

I always turn MINUS feedback into PLUSPLUS comments, so the people receiving it, like Sonia, don't begin to think in terms of what they did wrong; instead, they think about how they can do it better next time.

Examples of MINUS versus PLUSPLUS feedback:

MINUS	PLUSPLUS
You spoke too fast.	You could've spoken more deliberately.
I missed some pauses.	You could've used a few more pauses.
I didn't like your hectic movements.	If you exercise more control over your movements on stage, you'll project more authority.
You use too many filler sounds, like "um" and "ah".	You could convert those filler sounds you use, like "um" and "ah", into very effective pauses instead.
You are an emotional refrigerator.	If you'd open up more and share your emotions, you'd connect much more with your audience.

It was the magic of PLUSPLUS, the approach that emphasizes "What you can do even better!" that turned Sonia into an outgoing, confident, passionate and persuasive communicator in just two days.

In this book you'll learn about more than a hundred PLUSPLUS patterns I've detected over the years — patterns for better communication.

You can use this book in a variety of ways:

As a business presenter, you can enhance your content, your delivery, and your slides.

As a salesperson, you can optimize your sales pitch.

As a Toastmaster, you can improve your evaluations.

This book discusses public speaking. And consider: it's *always* public speaking, whether you're speaking to a single person or in front of an audience of a thousand people.

Many of the PLUSPLUS patterns in this book also apply to your everyday communication, one-on-one, both in business and in your personal life.

You too can improve the same way Sonia did. After two days of receiving PLUSPLUS feedback and applying PLUSPLUS patterns, she said:

On Friday I was on the other side of the river. You brought me over to this side.

CONTENT, DELIVERY, SLIDES

This book focuses on three areas for improving your speeches and presentations — content, delivery, and slides. You'll learn about "boosters" and "brakes" in all three areas.

"Boosters" are PLUSPLUS patterns that will improve the quality of your communication if you use them more often.

"Brakes" are also PLUSPLUS patterns, but it will improve the quality of your communication if you *avoid* them.

Here are a few examples:

	BOOSTERS	BRAKES
CONTENT	Rhetorical Devices	Message Reducers
DELIVERY	Holograms	The Giggle
SLIDES	Speak and Click	Bullets

I. CONTENT

CONTENT BOOSTERS

PLUSPLUS PATTERNS THAT WILL IMPROVE YOUR SPEECHES
AND PRESENTATIONS EVERY TIME YOU APPLY THEM.

THE ACTION STARTS WITH AN ACTION

Once I attended an MBA class given by my friend Professor Conor Neill from the renowned IESE Business School in Barcelona. With gravity in his voice he addressed his class:

Ladies and gentlemen, please pay good attention. You will now hear the eight words that are most important to any public speaker.

The serious tone of Conor's voice immediately had the students grabbing their pens. Conor continued:

The eight most important words, for any public speaker, are: After listening to my speech, the audience will _____ !

Will what? What will they do? What action will they take? What action, real or symbolic, will people perform after they've listened to me?

Conor calls it "Point X", that one symbolic action that turns a passive listener into a committed follower.

Knowing more about my topic is not an action. Feeling more passionate about my cause is not an action. Signing my petition to save the orangutans in Borneo — that is an action.

I was sitting in a street café in Barcelona one afternoon, when suddenly a kindly looking lady in her late 50s approached me with a petition to save the famous orangutans of Borneo. Frankly, I'm not the number one petition-signer in the world, but this particular cause meant something to me. Rose, my beloved, my special rose, comes from Sabah, in Borneo, home of the orangutan. So I signed.

Two weeks later I received a phone call:

Mr. Mueck, you have signed a petition here to help save the orangutan....

Now — what were the chances that I'd have just put the phone down? Normally, they're about 99½%, like when a telephone solicitor calls me to sell me a better wireless connection.

But I couldn't do that, because I'd already committed myself. That tiny little symbolic action of signing that petition had an amazing amount of persuasive power. It made me feel a sense of personal obligation.

Most of the speakers I've ever heard haven't included a concrete call to action. There hasn't been a "Point X" — which means that significant opportunities have been missed!

The first content-boosting action to take in the future is to write down these eight words, then to come up with a concrete action for your audience to take once they've listened to your speech or presentation.

It's the very first step. Once you've defined your Point X, you're ready to move on.

Boost your content even more by demanding a symbolic action from your audience.

ONE SPEECH, ONE THEME

Our company is a great adventure.

A speech that starts with such a metaphorical theme can only be good. It's always great to use a theme throughout your speech. Good themes are those that everyone in the audience can easily relate to: a journey, a rollercoaster ride, marriage, a building, a thunderstorm, the gym, football, a marathon.

A metaphorical theme is more memorable than an abstract concept. Staying with the example above — what makes an adventure an adventure?

In an adventure you have heroes: the sales guys in the company, the management, the IT team.

In an adventure you encounter obstacles: competition, regulation, recession.

In an adventure you take risks: a new product launch, a new market entry, a joint venture.

Your audience will appreciate such a theme. They can identify with it; they can visualize it; they can feel it.

Make sure you don't mix themes in a speech. Mixed metaphors are too confusing for your audience. Stick to one theme.

Boost your content even more by using a single metaphorical theme throughout your speech.

A GREEK TEMPLE WITH THREE PILLARS

Imagine you're sitting in an audience listening to a speech. Why would it be important for you that the speech have a good structure?

Now — imagine you are giving a speech in front of an audience. Why would it be important for you as a speaker to have a good structure?

Good structure is crucial for both the speaker and the audience. The speaker wants to stay on track, avoid forgetting important parts, keep the logical flow moving. The listener wants to follow the speaker's points — and the easier that is, the better.

Good structure boosts the quality of your content.

A simple and powerful model for structuring your speeches is the Speech Structure Building™ model, as I explained in *The Seven Minute Star*[2].

The Speech Structure Building™ is a model of a Greek temple: it has a foundation (the speech's opening), three pillars (the body: points A, B, C), and a rooftop (the closing). What makes this model special is the "drainpipe" which connects the roof with the foundation.

Example: a speech about "The future of Europe"

It was the best year of my life. One year of freedom, one year of friendship, one year of Europe – it was my Erasmus exchange year in Barcelona, 1997-98. Ever since then, I've been a passionate European, and I'll give you three powerful reasons why Europe has a great future ahead.

First, our infrastructure. Look at the ports of Rotterdam, Hamburg, Barcelona. Look at the airports of Frankfurt, Paris, Madrid. Look at the

---

2 Available from Amazon.com and other retailers

highways in Poland or Hungary. We have top-notch infrastructure in Europe – a prerequisite for successful global business operations.

Second, our culture. Europe is a superbly attractive place to work and live for global-quality people. Our art, our cuisine, our fashion, our films, our music, our sports — Europe offers culture and lifestyle at its best.

The third, and from my perspective the most powerful reason for a bright European future, is our political system. It's a system based on freedom, equal rights, and democracy. This is the system I want for my son Álvaro, when he grows up. This system guarantees stability and growth for the coming generations.

Today I'm back in Barcelona, a convinced European, back in the city of my Erasmus year. I've lived my personal European dream for the last decade; I live my European dream today, and I'll live it tomorrow as well. Europe is our future.

Opening — A – B – C — closing, with a connection back to the opening. Leonardo Da Vinci said that simplicity is the ultimate sophistication; follow his advice, and let your public speeches follow this simple structure. Be sophisticated and use the Greek temple: foundation, three pillars, roof, and the drainpipe.

Boost your content even more by using the Speech Structure Building™.

FIVE WAYS

In my seminars I usually ask a female participant about the amount of time she would grant to a guy who's obviously launching a flirtation attack. Most times — after the laughter, the red cheeks, and the jokes have died down — she'll say that she'd give a guy about 30 seconds.

If you are a male reader — well, I don't know about your experience, but mine doesn't even come close to 30 seconds.

Hello, my name is Flor... — Oh — well — ok — bye!

I don't even have time to get out my whole name. I've never experienced anything else but an average of 1.3 to 1.7 seconds.

For me, the same thing applies to public speaking. When you speak in public, when you present your product, when you give a eulogy, when you make a pitch for funding for your start-up company, when you give a best man's speech — always think about how you have 1.3 to 1.7 seconds to capture the attention of your audience.

With this in mind, here are five ways to start your next speech or presentation:

QUOTATION

A quotation from an admired personality is a safe way to start a speech. I recommend quotations that express the central, key message of your speech. Imagine a speech to a group of employees: *perseverance* might be the key to your message. Use Google, search for "quotation" and "perseverance", and you'll find a vast variety of useful quotations.

You could start a speech by saying,

Albert Einstein once said...

Pause! Let them picture the guy with the crazy white hair-do.

"It's not that I'm so smart, it's just that I stay with problems longer."

— I want us to stay with our problems longer than any competitor, I want

us to stay with our problems longer than any analyst expects from us, I want us to stay with our problems longer than any solution would ever require.

A neat side effect of starting with a quotation is that it awards you borrowed credibility and intellect right from the start.

POLEMIC

Our sector will drown...

This is a miserable situation...

Starting your speech with a polemic has an immediate impact, and will grab an audience's attention. I call it the *WHAT?* effect.

Hello, my name is Florian... — That lady in the back thinks, *Yeah, whatever!*

Our sector will drown... — Your audience thinks, *WHAT?*

Polemic openings are great; however, it's important to make sure you resolve them in a positive way — but only after a long, dramatic pause.

Our sector will drown... Pause! *...in a sea of success!*

This is a miserable situation... Pause! *...for pessimists. Again we outpaced our competition!*

Polemics are great attention-getters.

ONE WORD

Does your speech have a message? It had better. Without a message you have no speech; you have nothing to present. Now — you can reduce any message in the world to one word.

Take the Albert Einstein example from above: Perseverance.

Personally, I love the one-word start because of its radical simplicity. Once expressed with dignity and intonation, your portentous word hums in the room, and everyone in your audience knows, after just 1.3 seconds, what your presentation will be about.

A participant in one of my seminars once started his speech by saying,

Divorce....

An uncanny silence blanketed the room; we all felt smothered by a blanket of negativity. It didn't even take him 1.3 seconds to capture our fullest attention.

QUESTION

Rhetorical or not, questions are always a great tool for getting your audience to listen to what you are about to say.

Have any of you guys ever been to Barcelona?

What would you picture in your mind if you heard this question? Isn't it hard not to picture the Sagrada Familia, F.C. Barcelona, or the beautiful sandy beaches? Even those who have never been will search their memories for anything they might have heard about Barcelona — Gaudí, perhaps, or the 1992 Olympics.

Whether we verbalize an answer or not, we will always be alert to questions. Questions make us think. Always remember, a thinking audience is a good audience — unless you're a politician!

PERSONAL ANECDOTE

Sharing a personal anecdote at the beginning of your speech that shows why you're passionate about your cause will automatically increase the level of your ethos[3], the credibility you convey as a speaker.

Imagine you want to persuade your audience to become entrepreneurs. You could start your speech by saying:

The room was always full. I remember that our classrooms at university were always overcrowded — but not because of me! I would be sitting at home, in the students' residence, launching my first entrepreneurial adventures, together with my friend Dennis.

I may not be Michael Dell; I'm certainly not Bill Gates. But I tried; therefore, I do have the credibility to talk about entrepreneurship.

When you start your speech or presentation with a story or anecdote that boosts the level of your personal ethos, step by step you wade more deeply into the waters of persuasiveness.

Boost your content by taking an unbreakable hold upon your audience's attention; begin your speech with a quotation, a polemic, a single portentous word, a question, or a personal anecdote.

---

3 Ethos: Greek for "credibility". Ethos, logos (reason) and pathos (emotion) are the three pillars of rhetoric.

WELCOME AND THANKS

But I can't start my speech with one of those five patterns. I have to welcome the dignitaries and authorities and thank the organizers first.

I hear this all the time. Yes, some events and occasions require a welcome, and thanking certain people and institutions. But my question is:

Have you ever tried to do it differently?

Only dead fish swim with the flow. I don't want to be a dead fish. I want to capture the full attention of every last seat in my audience in the first 1.3 to 1.7 seconds.

Imagine these opening words:

Dear Mr. President, dear Madam President, honored Dean and Professors, honored guests and friends of this institution....

Would words like these ever capture an audience's full attention? *Ever?*

Instead, by this time the last three rows have already fallen asleep.

You can do better. You can change the order of things. You can welcome the dignitaries and thank the organizers *after* your opening lines.

Example: a "Commencement address"

It was a rainy November evening 18 years ago. A new chapter of my life was about to begin. 1,000 anxious eyes gathered in this very same room; mine were among them. Doubt and anticipation met and mingled. What would my future bring? What would it look like? Would I become the CEO of Siemens? Would I start my own venture? My future was draped in fog, but now my present is clearly in my sight. What made the fog disappear?

Dear Mr. President, dear Madam President, honored Dean and Professors, honored guests and friends of this institution...

There are no rules in public speaking. You make the rules. You can change the expected order of things to increase the impact of your speech. No one is going to come up to you at the cocktail party later and say,

You didn't follow protocol!

(And if someone does, just smile, chuckle indulgently, and turn away.)

Boost your content even more by grabbing the audience's attention straightaway, and then doing the welcoming and thanking.

WHAT IS IT ALL ABOUT?

Have you ever attended a talk by a speaker who just talks and talks and talks, but you haven't a clue about where the whole thing is going?

It's important that your audience know the main point of your speech or presentation very early on. If they haven't learned it after about a minute, they'll rapidly start getting uneasy.

My recommendation for you is to mention your key message, the point of your talk, at the end of your introduction.

Example: a speech about "Friendship"

Have you ever missed your friends when you needed them most? Have you ever let a good friend down? Have you ever cried for a friend you lost?

Friends are one of the most valuable treasures we have in life. Today I want to encourage you to invest more time into this treasure.

From that point onward you present your arguments and reasons, stories and anecdotes. But your audience will know right from the start what your speech is all about.

Boost your content even more — cement your key message in the audience's mind by mentioning it by the end of your introduction.

GOOD-BETTER-BEST

Think about one of your favorite movies. Think about one of your favorite books. Is there a climax in "Star Wars"? Is there a climax in "The Usual Suspects"? Is there a climax in "Perfume"?

Apart from "Pulp Fiction" — a movie with at least 534 climaxes — good movies and novels, and even New Yorker articles, have a climax.

Climax, a rhetorical device, is based on the good–better–best structure. I'm frequently amazed that so few people exploit this dramaturgic tool.

Why would you speak first about the passion of your employees, but then conclude with a detailed exposition of the company's IT infrastructure? Believe it or not, there are people who do.

From now on, especially in the body of your talk (the three pillars of your Speech Structure Building™), you'll want to use a structure that includes a climax.

A = GOOD   B = BETTER   C = BEST

Example: on "The benefits of Barcelona"

What I really like about Barcelona is the weather. We have an average of 300 sunny days a year in Barcelona, and, considering how important sunshine is to our well-being, it's no wonder people walk around smiling all the time.

What's even better about the Catalan capital is its cosmopolitan lifestyle. People from all over the world come together for tapas, business, or Toast-masters meetings.

For me, the absolute best of Barcelona is the beach. Very few major cities in the world can boast a four mile long sandy beach right near the center of town. After a tough day, sitting at a beach bar at night listening to chillout music and sipping a fine Priorat by the light of flickering torches is simply priceless.

The climax structure works in the body of your speech, and smaller climaxes will work for a certain number of shorter points in your talk (within the A-B-C pillars). Always move up the ladder of excitement. Your audience will be thrilled, waiting to hear what's even better than what came before.

Boost your content even more by building at least one climax into your speech.

FROM CATERPILLAR TO BUTTERFLY

A caterpillar turns into a cocoon. A cocoon turns into a butterfly. These two evolutionary steps happen with smooth transitions. You can tell that a change is happening, although you may well be surprised by the result.

Many public speakers underestimate the importance of good transitions between the parts of their speeches. Many don't use transitions at all, which is guaranteed to make for a bewildered audience. Where does one part end; where does the next part begin? Without transitions, the audience can't follow the flow, the logical argumentation, of the speech.

In the Speech Structure Building™ I strongly emphasize smooth and clear transitions.

Here are some generic examples of logical transitions:

Apart from A there is also B.

Now that we have discussed issue A, let's take a look at issue B.

What connects A and B is C.

Where does this lead? To B.

A is not the only aspect. B is also an important factor.

Here are some examples of more creative, not necessarily logical, transitions:

After a long pause, move to different position on the stage.

Show the titles of A, B, and C on sheets of paper, like in a boxing ring.

Recite a short poem between each speech block.

Your creativity is only limited by your imagination. Nothing is impossible in public speaking. Or are you a dead fish?

Boost your content even more by creating smooth and clear transitions.

THE DRAINPIPE

According to the 2009 World Champion of Public Speaking, Mark
Hunter of Australia, it's not the foundation that makes the Speech
Structure Building™ special. Neither is it the three A-B-C pillars — the
speech body. Nor is it the rooftop, which caps the three pillars, com-
pleting the Greek temple form of the Speech Structure Building™.

Mark says, *It's the drainpipe.*

The key element of this speech structuring model is the drainpipe,
which connects the closing of a speech with its opening.

Two examples of drainpipes:

Szymon from Krakow spoke in one of my seminars about his greatest
fears in life. He held a balloon in his left hand. He moved gently
towards one of his colleagues. Then – BOOM – the balloon burst right
in front of her face. Szymon yelled,

What did you see in her face?

Fear! shouted another colleague.

Szymon replied: *Exactly — fear!*

What a great opening!

But – when his speech came to an end, Szymon missed out on a great
opportunity to use a drainpipe. His message was that we should
change our perception about what we fear, that fear only exists in our
heads.

In the feedback round after Szymon's speech, I suggested that he could have picked up another balloon and, without bursting it, passed it to the same colleague, and said, *Change your perception!*

That balloon would have made a magnificent drainpipe by connecting back to his beginning.

On another occasion my friend, conflict mentor Tobias Rodrigues, used a wonderful drainpipe based on chiasmus, a rhetorical device of reversed repetition. It was his icebreaker (his first speech) at our Toastmasters club in Barcelona.

Tobias opened his speech with the words, *My life in your hands....* He reinforced the phrase by using hand gestures — from touching his chest to reaching out to his audience.

Tobias ended his speech by saying, *Your hands in my life....*

As he said this, he reversed his hand gestures.

I just loved Tobias' chiastic drainpipe.

It's the drainpipe which makes your speech round, that brings it full circle. And — as you can see by the two examples, there are no limits to the creative possibilities when it comes to drainpipes.

Boost your content even more by constructing a drainpipe.

WHY SHOULD THEY CARE?

You can have the best content, the best delivery, the best slides, the best sound system, the best moderator to set the stage for you, and the friendliest audience. But if your speech is not relevant to your audience, it's nothing but a *dud*.

Why should people care about your message, about what you have to say?

This question should always be in the forefront of your mind. Most public speakers write their content, present it, and hope somebody will care. That's exactly *backwards!*

Instead, you should analyse your audience in advance, think about their needs, and adapt your speech content to those needs. Empathize with them; think about your audience's perspective, about how they feel. This will allow you to make your speech relevant to them.

A good way to boost your level of relevance is to ask rhetorical questions. Have you ever asked yourself why rhetorical questions are so powerful? Rhetorical questions make the audience confirm your point. Once they nod, indicating their agreement, you have them in the palm of your hand.

Who of you here has children? Aren't they wonderful? Aren't they precious? Wouldn't you agree that we should protect our little angels?

Today, I will talk about a budget increase for private security services.

Without the rhetorical questions, the audience might think only about the cost, and switch you off right away. On the other hand, after you've asked these rhetorical questions, it is very difficult for your audience just to tune you out. You've made it relevant to them personally.

Whether you use rhetorical questions or not, you must always find an answer to this one crucial question when you're preparing a speech: Why should they care?

Boost your content even more by making your speech relevant to your audience.

BE A MANDELA, BE A KING, BE A KENNEDY

The unification of a nation, equal rights, or a man on the moon — Nelson Mandela, Martin Luther King, and John F. Kennedy — they had one thing in common: they all shared their vision with the people.

How can you convince people to follow your lead if you don't share your vision? From business presentations to wedding speeches — always share your vision. Audiences love it.

Typical vison-triggering phrases are:

Where do I see this department five years from now?
My vision of the future is...
Imagine what we can accomplish as a team...

Once I visited the Hewlett-Packard plant in Barcelona. In a long hallway, a mega-sized poster said: *Seeing is believing.* With your personal vision, you paint a colorful picture of the future. People can see it, and they can start to believe in it. If you don't share your vision, you'll miss out on a great opportunity to communicate. Maybe you're not a Mandela or a King or a Kennedy, but you have a vision too. Share it with your audience!

Boost your content even more by sharing your vision.

ONCE UPON A TIME

Back in the days when there were no iPads, no cell phones, no comput-
ers, no television, back in the days when radio didn't even exist, back in
those days the epitome of communication was the storyteller.

We humans love stories. We love to hear stories; we love to tell stories.
Hence, it's only common sense to tell stories in speeches. But, as
Voltaire put it: *Common sense is not so common.* Most public speakers
completely forget about telling stories.

One of my clients is a European market leader in distributing frozen
food. In a seminar I asked a bunch of the sales guys about their competi-
tive advantage. Without thinking, and in unison, they replied:

We have the integrated frozen food chain.

Now, I've played baloney-bingo myself (I was a business consultant for
almost a decade), so I thought, *What a great blah-blah phrase!* I wanted
to know more about it.

During our lunch break my clients explained their integrated frozen food
chain to me. I learned about a Swedish farmer named Mr. Mallmö, who
grows peas. A driver picks them up, and in less than two hours the fresh
product has been flash-frozen. After they've been packaged, the peas are
delivered to sales centers throughout Europe — one of them in Kamp-
Lintfort, close to Düsseldorf. Thomas Müller is a driver there. His
client, the 92 year-old Mrs. Theissen, sometimes orders peas. When she
does, Thomas drives to her home and walks up to the fourth floor
carrying the peas in a special box. Thomas Müller usually chats about
life for a while with Mrs. Theissen, before he takes the peas to her
freezer, opens the door, and places them on the shelf. From a Swedish
field to Mrs. Theissen's freezer — an integrated frozen food chain.

I looked at them, frowned, and asked, *Why don't you tell that story instead?*

Stories connect with people much more than fancy marketing expressions ever could. As you've already learned, personal anecdotes and stories make a great opening, so you can connect right from the start.

Once I gave an inspirational speech at the Berlin-based web conference Heureka! 550 people out there in front of me, poor acoustics with a severe echo, and high expectations. It was then that I experienced the power a personal anecdote can have as a speech opener:

Last Tuesday morning I woke up in our home in Bigues i Riells, a small mountain village on the outskirts of Barcelona. I woke up because someone was licking my hand. It was Lucas — our Golden Retriever.

I turned around to give Rose, my sweetheart, a good-morning hug, but then I remembered that she was on a business trip to Madrid.

So I got up, went to the kitchen, and made myself some coffee. I opened the computer, checked my Twitter account, then had my first sip of coffee.

I got dressed and went out. It was a sunny day — as usual. I went to the mailbox to pick up the mail, and that one letter caught my attention in an instant. I rushed back to the kitchen, dropped the other letters, opened the envelope, unfolded the letter, and thought — Heureka!

You should've seen them. Without saying anything, but building suspense, I managed to get everyone in the entire room listening to me, right from the start. It was fantastic!

It's a good idea to begin your stories at a particular moment in the past, like *last Tuesday morning* or *two months ago.* That signals that a story is coming, and your audience will be hooked right away.

Your life is full of the greatest stories you could possibly tell. Tell as many stories as possible. And the best thing? These stories are already in your head. You don't even need to use notes.

Boost your content even more by telling stories.

THE SIX-WORD STORY

Ernest Hemingway, the famous American writer, was a master of packing a great deal of meaning into just a few words. He became famous for his compelling short stories, such as *The Killers* (1927). Later he wrote such masterpieces as *For Whom The Bell Tolls, The Old Man And The Sea,* and *The Sun Also Rises.*

Once a friend challenged Hemingway to come up with a short story of only six words. Never short of self-esteem, Hemingway took on the challenge. The result is impressive:

For sale: baby shoes, never worn.

With only six words Hemingway manages to drive our imagination into the wildest directions. It's an art to say less but express more.

Public speakers tend to do exactly the opposite. They talk more and say less. They have difficulty getting to the point, or they never hit their target at all.

Less is more — it's the golden rule of public speaking.

If you changed your job because you didn't get along with your boss, there's no need to explain that conflict-laden relationship in detail — that he never really liked you because you voted for the wrong political party, and on top of that, he tried to hit on your wife at the Christmas party, but she wasn't interested and he couldn't cope with the rejection, and — and — and —

You get the point? All you need to say is that you changed jobs because you and your boss didn't get along. Less is more.

It's like Cinderella, who separates the good peas from the bad peas. Look for words and phrases that resonate with meaning. Every word counts in public speaking, and every word less counts more.

Boost your content even more by talking less and saying more.

A BUNCH OF RED, YELLOW AND ORANGE FLOWERS

When you tell stories in a speech, be very descriptive.

You could say, *She gave me a bunch of flowers.*

Or you say, *She gave me a bunch of red, yellow and orange spring flowers.*

You could say, *I crossed the street.*

Or you say, *I crossed the dimly lit street.*

You could either say, *A friend of mine from the UK.*

Or you could say, *A college buddy of mine from Bristol, with whom I shared a room and some of the best days of my life.*

As public speakers we can learn from great novelists like Thomas Mann, Ernest Hemingway or Charles Dickens. Be more descriptive; add color to your speech content. Play with the imagination of your audience.

Boost your content even more by being more descriptive.

THEY HAVE FIVE SENSES

We can hear. We can see. We can smell. We can taste. We can feel the things we touch and that touch us. People have five senses. A great way to boost your storytelling is to trigger all five senses of your audience.

What most public speakers do well is appeal to people's visual sense:

Suddenly I was standing in front of this imposing Gothic church.

And then a sleazy businessman in his early fifties approached me.

I was standing in front of the cheesiest Chrismas tree I had ever seen.

What you can do even better in public speaking is to activate all the other senses — hearing, touch, smell and taste.

Examples: "Hearing"

I heard a squeeking sound.

We listened to the song "With Or Without You" by U2.

The deep growl of an accelerating Harley-Davidson woke me up.

Examples: "Touch"

The skin of the great white shark felt like sandpaper.

I touched the hot iron.

The fine white sand of the Seychelles beach slipped softly through my fingers.

Examples: "Smell"

My neighbor's freshly baked Streusel cake reminded me of happy days in my childhood.

It smelled like conference coffee.

A choking black cloud of diesel smoke enveloped us.

Examples: "Taste"

It tasted like crispy Oktoberfest chicken.

I will never forget the fruitfully acid taste of that 2004 Numantia red wine.

The peach was so ripe it tasted like innocence.

The senses of hearing and smell offer the most pregnant possibilities for distinguishing yourself from other speakers. Songs, sounds, and smells, blended and seasoned, make a fantastic rhetorical dish.

Boost your content even more by touching all five senses of your audience.

"I", NOT "ONE"

Storytelling needs to be personal. When we talk about difficult times in life, weaknesses, failures, or other topics that make us uneasy, we tend to switch from the personal "I" form to the impersonal "you" or "one" form.

Example: "Subway ticket"

When you become an entrepreneur and face economic thunderstorms, it could happen that you find yourself standing in front of the ticket machine at a subway station, and suddenly you realize — you cannot even pay for a ticket.

But — you connect much better with your audience when you use the "I" form:

My symbolic moment of perseverance arrived as I was standing at the Rosenthaler Platz subway station in Berlin. All my credit cards were blocked, and I had 1.27 € left in my pocket. I couldn't afford a simple subway ticket. I felt humiliated.

Take all your impersonal statements and make them personal:

From: *One feels badly when being bullied.* To: *I felt badly when they bullied me.*

From: *One should never give up.* To: *I never gave up.*

From: *One must believe.* To: *I needed to believe.*

Boost your content even more by personalizing what you say.

THEY HAVE A NAME

Another area that improves our storytelling involves the way we use names. In my seminars, most speakers talk about a client, about their children, about their spouses, bosses, neighbors, or colleagues.

But — they almost never give these people names.

You make your stories more personal when you use people's names:

My ex-boss, mentor, and friend Ralf Beunker...

My son Álvaro...

Daniel Braun, a client-friend of mine...

It's easy to fix this. Use names throughout your entire speech. You'll sound much more personable, and you'll sound like you're more grounded in the real world.

Boost your content even more by giving people names.

AND THEN MY DAD SAID

I'm a great fan of dialogs in public speeches. When it comes to drama, however, most people are reluctant. *I'm not an actor*, they say. The reality is, they're shy and self-conscious — so they need some encouragement!

The truth is: you don't have to be an actor. As my friend, professional speaker Olivia Schofield, says, *An actor is an expert at being someone else, while, as a public speaker, you're an expert at being yourself.*

You can still add some significant, effective drama to your speeches — easily. You can spice up your content by using dialogs.

And then my dad said: Son, you know what makes me the happiest man on earth? When I'm out on the street and see a group of my alumni after 30 years, and the first thing I see on their faces when they see me is a smile. That makes me the happiest man on earth.

When we use dialogs, we change our facial expression, we vary our voice, we use dramatic acting techniques — and we're not even aware we're doing it.

When I speak about the power of a smile, I always recall this conversation with my dad. I remember him; I see him; I feel him. This is why that dialog comes across as authentic — because it was *real*.

Dialogs with moms and dads are always great, because almost all of us have them. Almost everyone can identify.

Many other conversations are easy to remember and use as dialogs — with other family members, friends, partners, teachers, bosses, colleagues, suppliers, clients, shopkeepers, bartenders — the list is endless.

If your audience speaks a certain type of jargon, and you want to connect with them on a more casual level, dialogs can also serve as a smart carrier of what might otherwise be inappropriate expressions:

Then my friend Thomas replied, "This is crap!"

You didn't say it — your friend Thomas did!

Dialogs bring life into your speeches, and bring your speeches to life. Use them often!

Boost your content even more by adding dialogs.

A GREAT CONNECTOR

A special form of dialog is the internal dialog, also known as "soliloquy".

I always wondered, Can I really do this?

I asked myself, Am I doing the right thing?

For years I looked for an answer to this question: Shouldn't I go for a big change in my life?

This pattern has popped up in countless speech evaluations. Internal dialog connects with your audience. The reason is simple: Humans have doubts, anxieties, wishes, longings, unanswered questions. When you launch a dialog with yourself, your audience can easily identify with you.

Boost your content even more by including a soliloquy.

THE PASSION BRIDGE

How can I present the monthly business unit results with passion?

I've heard this question, or something similar, so many times — and I have to admit, the question makes a valid point. And yet, making excuses for dull public speeches correlates 100% with a lack of creativity.

You can, literally, add passion to any speech. The trick is to use the passions and hobbies of your life, and build metaphorical bridges to your speech content. You'll find that a great many metaphorical bridges lead right into the heart of the language of business:

Chess: vision, planning, strategy

Children: growth, motivation, lifelong learning

Cooking: vision, patience, creativity, innovation

Cycling: perseverance, the extra mile, training

Fishing: market analysis, promotion, patience

Friends: trust, reliability, "client" orientation

Marathon: perseverance, milestones, strategic focus

Mountain climbing: risk taking, goal setting, teamwork

Piano: multitasking, versatility

Soccer: team play, training, strategy and tactics

What are your passions and hobbies in life? Use them! You can build metaphorical bridges to all kinds of content — even to that presentation of your business unit's monthly results.

A software company's major markets were Spain, Germany, the UK, France and Italy. So when the CFO presented the finance department's strategy, he used the UEFA Champions League[4] as his metaphor. He gave their key clients the names of famous football clubs: F.C. Barcelona, Bayern München, Manchester United, Olympique Lyonnais, AC Milan. Since he was himself such a fervent football fan, his passion powered his presentation so much that his eyes sparkled as he explained his strategy and virtually scored his future goals.

Nothing is impossible in public speaking. Using your passions creatively makes for more effective presentations.

Boost your content even more by building bridges of passion.

---

4 The most prestigious soccer competion in Europe on a club level.

FEELINGS, FEELINGS, FEELINGS

Aristotle's *On Rhetoric*, written in classical Greek, is a treatise on the art of persuasion dating from the 4th century BCE. In it, the great philosopher describes the three pillars of rhetoric: logos (reason), ethos (credibility), and pathos (emotion).

The last, pathos, presents an especially difficult hurdle for most speakers. *In The Seven Minute Star,* I explained the importance of building bridges of sympathy with the audience. Here, "pathos" does not imply "pathetic"; rather, it's more related to "sympathy" and "empathy". Pathos is necessary to persuade people and move them to action.

Analyze the following two paragraphs. Which of them connects more with you?

Alternative A:

After I graduated from college, I went to live and work in the States for two years. For the first time of my life I lived far away from home.

Alternative B:

After I graduated from college, I went to live and work in the States for two years. For the first time of my life I lived far away from my family. Sometimes, when I missed my parents and my little sister, I felt lonely.

My friend Peter Zinn, from the Netherlands, is a passionate public speaker who occasionally gives workshops on storytelling. He has a great way to point out the difference between logic and emotions.

First, Peter holds up a tennis ball and says, *This is our logical brain.*

Then, he holds up a huge beach ball in his other hand and remarks, *And this is our emotional brain. Both brains are important. But if they're in conflict, guess which one of them will win?*

We connect much more with people if we connect with them on an emotional level. Therefore, add pathos to your speeches and presentations. Add feelings. There are many ways you can feel.

There are feelings of anger. Then you feel frustrated, hurt, furious, disgusted, embarrassed or jealous.

There are feelings of uneasiness. Then you feel nervous, anxious, confused, weak, foolish or stupid.

There are feelings of fright. Then you feel miserable, trapped, scared, terrified or lonely.

There are other negative feelings. Then you feel distrustful, suspicious, bitter, paranoid or resentful.

Then, there are feelings of happiness. Then you feel pleased, hopeful, proud, excited, overjoyed or loved.

When you write your speeches, check those lists of emotions on Google. You will find plenty of them. Add pathos — feelings — to your speeches. Aristotle will be proud of you.

Boost your content even more by sharing your feelings.

WHY YOU?

While pathos is the emotional appeal to your audience, ethos is the credibility you have as the bearer of a message. Why should your audience believe you and not someone else? What makes you a point of reference for a certain topic? What is the source of your wisdom?

I give many seminars to the online industry, so I've gotten to know many engineers, coders, and hackers. I like to ask them about their first contact with a PC. During a workshop in Berlin I asked Thomas about the first experience he ever had with a computer.

He told me that he was about eight years old, playing with his toys, when his father came into his room. In his hands he had a box all giftwrapped. It was his birthday present. Filled with anticipation, Thomas ripped the wrapping off his present. The big letters on the box read, "Commodore Amiga 500".

Ever since that day Thomas was hooked on PCs and programming. I told Thomas, who regularly speaks at IT conferences, to blend this personal anecdote into every talk he gives, because this Amiga 500 story powers up Thomas' level of ethos. It makes him a more credible source of information and persuasion.

What makes you a great programmer, a great banker, a great business consultant, a great social worker, a great nurse? What are your early experiences with your profession, or with your topic of choice? Refresh your memory, and tell those stories in your speeches. You'll communicate with a great deal more credibility.

Boost your content even more by telling ethos-building anecdotes.

UNDEFEATED FOR 2,300 YEARS

I've played soccer with minor league clubs for more than 20 years, so whenever I can, I use a football metaphor. On my blog[5] I published a popular post about my favorite team of rhetorical devices. I call it "F.C. Rhetoric".

11 players, 11 content boosters. This team is not about winning a game. This team is not about winning a league. This team is about winning, persuading, motivating, and inspiring your audience. I encourage you to become a fan of F.C. Rhetoric and use these players in your own speechwriting as much as you can.

Who are the outstanding players on this extraordinary team?

1 ALLITERATION

Alliteration, the goalkeeper. He's not good, he's great! His saves are gargantuan. He always goes for gold!

2 ANAPHORA

Anaphora is the fastest player in the league. When Anaphora runs down the left wing, his opponents start to panic. When Anaphora runs down the left wing, the F.C. Rhetoric fans jump to their feet. When Anaphora runs down the left wing, the other team knows it's in big trouble.

3 CHIASMUS

Chiasmus is the poet of the team. He loves to cross — on and off the field. Once at a team retreat he started his birthday toast with the words, *My life in your feet.* He ended by saying, *Your feet in my life.*

---

5 www.florianmueck.com

4 CLIMAX

Climax is a good technical defender. Even better is his attitude — he never gives up. But what makes him the best central defender in the league is his spooky gift of anticipating passes.

5 EPIZEUXIS

The right wing defender, Epizeuxis, loves to practice, practice, practice, because only one thing matters: winning, winning, winning.

6 METAPHOR

Metaphor is an animal. When he runs, he is a leopard. For stamina, he is a horse. He has the eyes of an eagle.

7 ONOMATOPOEIA

Boom! Onomatopoeia snaps, crackles, and pops when he breaks out an attack in the midfield.

8 OXYMORON

The game of the team captain is of modest magnificence. The kindly arrogant Oxymoron is famous for his boldly humble statements at press conferences.

9 PARALIPSIS

Paralipsis holds the team record for red cards. He keeps badgering the defense with statements like, *I am not your father, to tell you that you are a loser!* Another favorite of his is: *I'm not even going to mention my enor-mous satisfaction for having scored three goals against you.* His coach says, *I'm not even going to talk about the way Paralipsis keeps getting into fights.*

10 PERSONIFICATION

When Personification dribbles the ball through enemy lines, the ball turns into a monster. It creeps and crawls, it jumps and tumbles; up on its feet, it marches inexorably toward its destiny — it's unstoppable. Goal!

11 RHETORICAL QUESTION

His comrades always make fun of his weird, double-barreled name. Yet Rhetorical Question is the great motivator of the team. At half-time, when they're losing, he'll get on a chair and shout at the rest of them, *After 2,300 years of sweat, after 2,300 years of tears, after 2,300 years of triumph — do we really want to lose this game? Are we going to let others experience the sweet taste of victory? Or will we go out there and fight like Leonidas and his men?*

11 fantastic players on your team, for your winning speech!

Of course, a winning team needs more than 11 players. 11 players win a game, but it's the bench and the substitutes who win the league.

At www.virtualsalt.com/rhetoric.htm you find all the substitute players of this great team, F.C. Rhetoric.

Boost your content even more by deploying the players of F.C. Rhetoric.

ALWAYS THREE

If you were the child of Susan Webber and Albert Einstein, and your IQ was 193 — how many different points could you remember in a speech of 30 minutes?

The answer is: seven or eight. Only the very most intelligent of the most intelligent people could remember more than a maximum of eight points. The regular educated crowd would be able to cope with five points. And remember, good memory and intelligence do not always correlate. The average audience can best remember three points. A golden rule of rhetoric is the rule of three.

Threes, triplets, triads — they're ubiquitous; just take a look around:

The iPAD 2? Slimmer, lighter, faster.

Donald Duck's nephews? Huey, Dewey, and Louie.

The Good, the Bad and the Ugly.

The ad slogan of the Paulaner beer brand? Good, better, Paulaner.

The three little pigs. The three bears. Three blind mice. Three wishes.

Marc Antony's famous line in Shakespeare's *Julius Caesar? Friends, Romans, and countrymen.*

It's because of this rule of three that the Speech Structure Building™ features three pillars: A – B – C.

If you brief an ad agency about your brand's equity, focus on the three most important factors. If you present a market study at a medical conference, outline the three most striking insights. If you sell your company's product, explain three characteristics and three benefits.

Always, always, always focus on three points in public speaking. What matters isn't what you know, it's what they can remember.

Boost your content even more by mentioning precisely three points.

OF VOLVOS AND FERRARIS

You've already met the midfield player of F.C. Rhetoric: Metaphor. Metaphor is a powerful stimulant of great speech content.

Seminar participant Claudio, when presenting the benefits of his company's antivirus software solution, mentioned two factors: speed and security. The words were written on a PowerPoint slide.

I created an alternative slide by replacing the words and their corresponding paragraphs with two simple images: a Ferrari, and a Volvo.

An image says more than a thousand words, but one word can also create a thousand images. Suppose my client had talked about the Ferrari and the Volvo in his speech. Wouldn't you feel the speed? Wouldn't the security feel comforting?

Images work in our minds much better than words. Replace your word-driven content with images, and set your audience's imagination on fire.

Example: "Life"

My life is a rollercoaster ride. It's had ups, it's had downs; it's gone slowly, it's gone fast; it's had fear, it's had laughter; it's had tears, it's had smiles. Sometimes I had to go through a loop-de-loop to pick up the pace. But just as with a rollercoaster, I'm enjoying the ride, and I'd do it over and over again.

Boost your content even more by painting pictures with words.

HIS NAME IS ABDUL

Public speakers have the great gift of failing to give concrete examples. They speak about clients, companies, cities, children, holidays, dinners, lunches, friends — the list is endless. What they do not use, when they speak, is specific names, specific incidents — concrete examples.

Our minds prefer concrete examples, just as they prefer concrete visual images. We connect far better with a single story or example than with general, abstract terms.

Once I spoke at a consulting firm about the importance of networking. I could have said that, as a networker, you should treat all people the same way, whether it's the CEO of a multinational or the cleaning staff of your own company. This would have been the normal, expected approach, but it wouldn't have been tangible to my audience. I wanted to give a concrete example instead — with a name and a face.

So at one point in my speech I asked those 71 highly educated and highly professional financial advisors:

Does anyone in this room know the name of that kind gentleman who opened the door of your car this morning when you arrived? Does anyone know the name of that same gentleman who opened the door of the hotel and greeted you with such a warm and welcoming smile? Does anyone know his name?

Silence. After a long, uncomfortable pause, I continued.

His name is Abdul. He's been living in Germany for 26 years. He has two children, and he comes from the Northern part of Islamabad. He is super, super supremely proud of what he has accomplished in his life.

Networking is not about collecting business cards, nor is it about short-term professional success. Networking is about having a passion for people. If you treat the CEO of a too-big-to-fail bank any different from the way you treat Abdul, then you need an attitude adjustment — right now.

Don't talk about companies, cities, children, holidays, dinners, lunches, or friends. Don't talk about your clients in the telecom, IT or health sector. Talk about one client — one who has a name, and who had a specific challenge that needed a specific solution. Always make it tangible for your audience.

Boost your content even more by giving concrete examples.

WHO SHOT J.R.?

Were you hooked on "24", the television series with Kiefer Sutherland? Or on "Dallas" back in the 80s? Or, even earlier, on the "Flash Gordon" series in the 50s?

Always, at the peak of the drama, the show would break off and say: *To be continued.* With these cliffhangers producers hoped to ensure the audience would return to see how the characters would resolve their dilemma.

You too can make use of this technique when you speak in public.

It's called "the hook". It happens in a speech when you put the audience right in front of the door of curiosity — but you don't open it.

Example: "The room"

It was a bright summer morning. Our village was slowly waking up. In the distance a rooster sent out his good-morning wishes. But apart from him — absolute silence. A loud silence! I got up and walked over to the bath-

room. Normally, the brass door-handle would give a little squeak; not that day. Silence, everywhere. Only that rooster in the distance.

I cracked open the door. No sound. I slipped through the crack. And there it was — through eyes clogged with sleep, I saw the most beautiful thing I'd ever seen in my life.

Three weeks later I received a phone call from my good friend Simon ....

Your audience is captured right from the start. They want to know what it was you saw. The women in your audience, especially, can hardly cope with the curiosity. They'll hang on your words breathlessly, until the end, when you resolve the story.

Add a hook to your talks. It will drive your audience nuts — just as the producers of "24", "Dallas" or "Flash Gordon" did so successfully to all of us. Just in the U.S., 85 million people wanted to know, who shot J.R.?

Boost your content even more by leaving your audience dangling on a hook of suspense.

OMG!

It was going to be a sad story. We knew it; we felt it. It was that resigned, melancholy tone in her voice. But we didn't know where she was going.

For two minutes she painted a picture of happiness — of happy plans, of a happy future with marriage and kids. We smiled.

Then came the OMG moment. She received that phone call on a sunny morning in May 2010. They told her that her boyfriend had driven into a tree, and that he was dead.

OMG — Oh My God!

From happy dreams, the story twisted to absolute agony. From there, she took us on a journey of recovery, climaxing in the rediscovery of happiness, thanks to her colleagues, thanks to her friends, thanks to us.

It was a sad story, but with a great twist, a positive outlook. And it was fantastically well told.

Good speeches have a twist. It doesn't have to be an OMG! moment. It can be an AH-HA! moment. Or a WHAT? Moment. What they all have in common is that the speech shifts, and goes in a completely different direction.

Think about the movie "Pulp Fiction". There's not one twist, but multiple twists. Tarantino knows how to keep his audience awake. You can do it, too.

Boost your content even more by twisting into different directions.

YOU CAN MAKE THEM LAUGH

Mark Twain said that all generalizations were false including that one. Let's make another exception! Everyone wants to laugh — you, your friends, your audience.

But — how can you make your audience laugh?

Shakespeare knew what he was talking about when he said, *Better a foolish wit than a witty fool.* My own father helped his own cause quite a bit with quick-wittedness during his eleven year stint as a carnival club president in Weidach, the Northern Bavarian village where I grew up. My dad loved to make fun of himself, which always got a good laugh.

But he never said the obvious thing; he preferred to say something unexpected, in a roundabout way. My father — my hero — was a funny guy, and his audiences showed their appreciation when they laughed.

Following in my hero's footsteps, I keep working at discovering humor patterns. Here are four that anyone can use:

PICK ON INDIVIDUALS

In my blog post "Why Must The Alpha Dog Fall?" I explained the humorous effect of engaging with the big shots in your audience.

Picking on individuals , big shot or not, is almost always a sure-fire way to get your audience laughing. I got to know a guy named Joshua once at a corporate team-building event. Joshua didn't smile. Ever. So I made it a point to engage with him during my presentation, and it got a quick smile out of him. It only lasted a millisecond, but that was enough. I exclaimed: *Wow, Joshua, you CAN smile!*

Of course his colleagues knew about his standard horizontal facial line. They almost fell off their chairs.

SAY THE UNEXPECTED

A classic humorous pattern comedians often use is to build up tension — that is, expectations — in a sentence or paragraph, and then resolve it in an unexpected way. Playing mental games with your audience is a safe way to provoke laughter.

In the fall of 2010, we held our Toastmasters Continental Europe conference in Barcelona. Adam Wern from Sweden won the Humorous Speech competition. He started his speech by telling everyone that after 30 seconds, he was going to say the f-word. And that he was very aware of the fact that it was absolutely politically incorrect to use the f-word. And that he didn't care at all.

Instantly, the tension among the audience was palpable. After 30 seconds Adam released a long *FFFFFFFFFFF —ellow Toastmasters!*

The audience roared.

LAUGH AT YOURSELF

Self-deprecation, self-mockery — it's an endlessly fertile field for humor.

In Wikipedia we read:

Self-deprecating humor relies on the observation of something negative about the person delivering the commentary. Many comedians use self-deprecating humor to avoid seeming arrogant or pompous, and to help the audience identify with them. In this way, the use of self-deprecating humor could be seen as an application of the rhetorical concept of ethos. This is a major component of the comedy of comedians such as [...] Woody Allen, David Letterman, Rodney Dangerfield, Conan O'Brien.

For most people on this planet, British humor is the peak of self-deprecation. At the same event where Joshua smiled for a millisecond, another speaker from the UK repeatedly made us laugh by saying, *I survived those cups of coffee, even though they were British cups of coffee.* Or, *I did this and that and this and that, hence you could say I'm an expert in none.* The additional irony of knowing that this guy is in fact an expert in his field made his statement completely hilarious.

When I'm abroad, I like to say, *Yes, I'm German — boring, efficient, alcoholic!*

Laugh at yourself and they will laugh with you.

BE POLITICALLY INCORRECT (SOMETIMES)

Politics, religion, sex — they're the taboo subjects of public speaking. Yet, like the forbidden fruit, they're so very tempting.

If you're going to go walking on thin ice, I highly recommend that you use smart humor. Adam Wern, the *FFFFFFFFFF*-man from Sweden, harvested another round of laughter in a subtle and smart way. After his intro line, he continued: *What are you laughing about? What did you think I was going to say?*

That is smart humor. Adam threw a curve ball of political incorrectness back at the audience, but there was no way for them to catch it.

One good trick to use is the rhetorical device *paralipsis*, the left-wing striker of F.C. Rhetoric. When you use paralipsis, you call attention to something by specifically saying that you're not going to mention it.

Once I gave a speech about the rap and hip hop culture. At one point I entered the minefield of the explicit lyrics most rap tunes use. I told my audience that it was not politically incorrect to perform a bit of an explicit tune — that it was a reflection of that specific culture. I kind of wrapped it up in a blanket of paralipsis. Then, facing shock and terror in their eyes, I started to rap. I can still hear the laughter today.

My recommendation is to stretch the rubber-band of political incorrectness as far as possible. This will make your audience laugh more than anything else — just make sure the band doesn't burst!

Picking on individuals, saying the unexpected, laughing about yourself, being politically incorrect — these are four patterns of humor everybody can learn, practice, and use.

I'm sure my dad, the hero, smiles down from heaven every time I make my audiences laugh. Knowing him, he would say, *Good job, son, but there is still a lot to learn.*

Thanks, Dad.

Boost your content even more by using patterns of humor.

YO SOY FLORIAN

Every time there are foreigners in my seminars, such as Moroccans in Germany or Swedes in Spain, I ask them to say something in their native language in their speeches.

It could be the opening line or a surprising line in the middle. The vast majority of people love languages. You always spice up your speech when you add some linguistic variety to it.

Audiences also generally enjoy it if you can use local dialects. Once on YouTube I saw Henry Cho, a Korean-American comedian who was born and raised in Tennessee. It was hilarious to hear him speaking with a strong Tennessee twang — and he had good fun with the disjunction.

I often use a little Upper Franconian dialect when I speak in German. (It's the German version of a country-bumpkin accent.) It always gets a good laugh.

If you speak a foreign language, or if you know how to speak in a distinct local dialect, use it — the audience will be delighted.

Boost your content even more by speaking in foreign languages and local dialects.

ACTIVE BEATS PASSIVE

I was asked by that woman to come over.

This special package was sent to me by my client.

My colleague was promoted by our boss.

Why do people speak in passive voice so often? Why don't they say:

That woman asked me to come over.

My client sent me this special package.

Our boss promoted my colleague.

This is an easy fix. *Always* speak in active voice, never in passive voice. Passive voice is impersonal, even dehumanizing; it seeks to avoid placing, or taking, responsibility; active voice is involved, energetic, committed, and responsible. Active always beats passive!

You want to move people to action, not to the waiting room.

Boost your content even more by using active phrases.

EXPENSIVE MEANS EXCLUSIVE

Every word counts in public speaking, and negative words will count against you. There are plenty of everyday phrases we use without thinking about the subconcious impact they cause in others.

In public speaking it's all about euphemisms. According to Merriam-Webster a euphemism is the substitution of an agreeable or inoffensive expression for one that may offend or suggest something unpleasant.

I hear quite often sentences like: *I work for this small agency.*

What will *small* mean to the person who hears this information? Small means unstable, lack of cash flow, no larger clients, struggling.

I'd prefer to say, *I work for an agile agency.* Apart from the alliteration, this expression conveys speed, enthusiasm, passion. I also like, I *work for a boutique agency.* The connotation is obvious.

Every word counts in public speaking. Don't call it cheap; call it affordable. Don't call it expensive; call it exclusive. Don't call it bad; call it improvable. Don't call it a problem; call it a challenge. Don't call it price; call it value.

A euphemism is not a lie; a euphemism is saying something in a more positive way. Use euphemisms throughout your speeches.

Boost your content even more by saying it in a more attractive way.

THE PUNK ROCKER OF RHETORIC

Once I had the distinct honor and pleasure of training 71 top Microsoft executives in using PowerPoint. Oh, the ironies of life!

It was a one-day communication training workshop for which the VP Marketing flew over from London. He gave the keynote presentation on powerful communication.

He shared some fascinating personal insights from his own career. But one point he made really got burned into my long-term memory chip.

He called it "sound bites". A sound bite is a phrase that ruthlessly sticks out of an otherwise gray mass of content; its effect is that it's easy to remember — in fact, it's difficult to forget.

As an example, he mentioned a phrase he and his colleagues used to use in the mobile-phone industry. They called themselves the *punk rockers of mobile phones.*

A seminar participant of my software-download client said his company wanted to be the *Spotify of software.*

The punk rockers of mobile phones, or the Spotify of software — ever since I heard these sound bites, I don't have a prayer of forgetting them. Use sound bites in your own speeches and presentations. Your audience will talk about them during the coffee break — and the best ones they'll remember for years.

Boost your content even more by including sound bites.

MATH MAKES MARVELOUS MESSAGES

Ever since I found out about the "trust equation"[6], I've become a great fan of using mathematical formulas in presentations.

Mathematical formulas are wonderful because they can help make a complex issue appear logical and easy to understand.

Take a look at the trust equation:

---

6   The Trusted Advisor; Maister, Green, Galford, 2010

How would you define trust? Trust is truly a complex topic. It's a maze, and it's easy to get lost in it, definitely. Maister, Green, and Galford studied the subject of trust for years, teasing out the factors that impact the trust building process in the service industry.

They came up with the trust equation:

$$T = (C + R + I) / SO$$

Trust equals Credibility PLUS Reliability PLUS Intimacy divided by Self-Orientation

It's easy to understand and it's easy to remember.

I was so inspired by the trust equation that I came up with an equation of my own. It's the "communication equation". I use it to convey the most important factors for great communication.

$$C = SC + M + I$$

Communication equals Self-confidence PLUS Message PLUS Impact

I wasn't very good at math in school, but I have learned that math makes marvelous messages.

Boost your content even more by expressing verbal concepts as mathematical formulas.

ROUND IS NEVER RIGHT

Which one of the following alternatives sounds more credible to you?

Alternative A:

Last year we achieved revenues in the gaming unit of $200 million.

Alternative B:

Last year we achieved revenues in the gaming unit of $205 million.

Don't round numbers feel suspicious? "200" feels like it was rounded up, but no one would think that about the number "205".

I'm not saying that you should never round numbers up or down. It would be awkward to present a number like "197.43 million".

What I do recommend is to always round up or down to uneven numbers. In the above case I would mention the number of $197 million. I would not round it up to 200.

Boost your content even more by mentioning uneven numbers.

FACTUAL PROOF

In one seminar an anonymous guy claimed to have attended the best high school in his home town. This seemed rather aggressive to me, and merely his own personal perception, so in the feedback round I asked him:

You said that you were a student at the best high school in your town. Just for the record, which third party source would back you up, that this is the truth?

He looked at me awkwardly. After a while he said:

But everybody knows this.

Dear public speaker: *Never* assume that "everybody knows" something. You need to prove your point with facts from credible sources. I'm not a lawyer, but I have a number of lawyers as friends. No evidence, no case.

Now, what could our friend have said? He could have cited the number of scholarships granted; he could have mentioned grade averages at graduation. In an imaginary world, he could even have mentioned the number of Nobel Prize winners his school had nurtured.

But he had none of this. He just said that he'd been graduated from the best high school in town.

Without facts, without proof, he had fallen into the trap of arrogance. Audiences despise speakers who claim to be the best — in any field — without being able to back it up.

Next time you want to claim to be part of the *best* organization, make the effort to mention some specific facts from a credible independent source as proof that your point is based on fact.

Boost your content even more by proving your points with facts obtained from credible outside sources.

SOCIAL PROOF

It's one thing to celebrate the high school you attended. It's even more critical to celebrate yourself directly.

I am always punctual.

I am good at what I'm doing.

I'm the most effective salesman in our company.

I'm a great dad.

I was a great student.

Don't you just love when people celebrate themselves? It's kind of pathetic, but still, most of us do it now and then. Maybe it's not such a big deal when you're hanging out in the bar with your friends — they've gotten used to it and like you anyway. But in public speaking, stay away from self-celebration.

There is a trick though. You can create an image of personal excellence without appearing arrogant or boastful. You can benefit from the concept of "social proof". As long as it's other people who are saying it, you're fine.

Our secretary says that I'm always punctual.

My boss says that I'm good at what I'm doing.

I'm the most productive salesman in the company — at least that's what my colleagues say.

My son Álvaro says I'm a great dad.

According to my professors, I was a great student.

When you celebrate yourself, make sure someone else is confirming it.

Boost your content even more by adding social proof to your self-celebration.

THE CREDIBILITY THIEF

You can steal credibility without being a thief. How? By adding quotations to your content. Public speakers are accustomed to using quotations. Nevertheless, has it never occurred to you that they always use the same sources?

It's always Gandhi, always Martin Luther King, always JFK, always Albert Einstein, always Nelson Mandela, always Mother Theresa, and so on.

To benefit from your audience's educational level, I recommend you also use some unknown sources of quotations once in a while. Such as a female Bulgarian writer. Or Jean Houston, an American lecturer. She is the author of one of my favorite quotations:

At the height of laughter, the universe is flung into a kaleidoscope of possibilities.

Isn't it wonderful? Audiences love to learn, but even more, they love it when they already know something they're being told is wise. Throw the 8 x 6 meter image of Jean Houston at the hotel wall, and you'll witness several nods of understanding in your audience — and they'll agree that you're as intelligent as they are.

Another *Be the change you want to see in the world?* Ok — been there, done that. I'm not asking you to erase all the familiar quotations from your list; rather, I want to encourage you to add some new voices to your portfolio of borrowed credibility.

What all public speakers should have is a repertoire of quotations they know by heart. Vision, leadership, goals, team, perseverance — these are generic subjects that apply to all sorts of business activities. In my seminars I encourage my people to learn by heart one quotation for each of these areas.

Examples:

Vision is the art of seeing what is invisible to others. — Jonathan Swift

Leadership is the art of getting someone else to do something you want done because he wants to do it. — Dwight D. Eisenhower

From a certain point onward there is no longer any turning back. That is the point that must be reached. — Franz Kafka

Individual commitment to a group effort — that is what makes a team work, a company work, a society work, a civilization work. — Vince Lombardi

Dripping water hollows out stone, not through force but through persistence. — Ovid

Learn five quotations by heart; it will make you a more credible speaker.

Boost your content even more by adding popular AND surprising quotations.

ASK QUESTIONS

Most of the speakers at business events begin by talking about themselves and their companies. The title of their standard opening slide is, About us. It seems to be etched in stone: all business presentations are required to start the same way.

Before I begin, I would like to share with you some information about our company.

When a speaker starts to celebrate his or her company, the audience thinks, *If I were really interested in your company, I'd check your website on my iPad. To be honest, I'm not really interested in egoistic self-celebration. Tell me something I want to know.*

But it's not only the opening of their presentations. Throughout their entire talk, many speakers tend to speak about their products, their services, their solutions, their political views, their visions, their goals, their marketing plans, their, their, their — It's all about them! As if I cared!

Such an egocentric approach is annoying at best. The protagonist should never be you. The protagonist should always be your audience.

A good way to make the audience feel appreciated and involved is to interact with them. There are three ways to do this.

First you can ask them closed questions.

Who's been to New York?

The audience, whether they want to or not, whether they've been to New York or not — in their minds they see the Empire State Building, Central Park, the Statue of Liberty, the New York Yankees.

Your audience cannot escape your questions, and questions make them think. Always remember, a thinking audience is a good audience.

It's better to avoid open questions, such as, *What do you think about the American health system?* These automatically lead to a bunch of distracting discussions in the audience, which will kill the flow of your speech.

A special form of question is the rhetorical question, the right-wing striker of team F.C. Rhetoric. Haven't you ever wondered why speakers ask rhetorical questions?

The chapter above, "Why should they care?" has given some examples. If you ask the right rhetorical questions, the vast majority of your audience will agree — either on the *Yes* or the *No* side.

Do you want a better work-life balance?

Depending on the audience, this question might lead them into a big fat *Yes!* If they agree, you have them on your side. This is the power of the rhetorical question — you invite your audience to get on your side of the issue. Once they've agreed with you, psychologically it's almost impossible for them to switch over to the opposite side.

Rhetorical or not, questions are a great way to interact with your audience. Questions keep them awake, let them feel included, let them feel they've been heard, and show that you care about them and what they think.

Boost your content even more by asking questions.

MAKE REFERENCES

I always try to get event organizers to let me be the third speaker. The third slot is the last opportunity to talk to an audience while they're still awake. PLUS, it gives me a great opportunity to listen to other speakers.

Whenever I hear about some common ground I share with another speaker, I'll make a note of it. For example, a project in Barcelona, or love of football, or playing a musical instrument.

Then, when it's my turn, I'll make apparently spontaneous references to the other speakers, using whatever it is that we have in common.

Like John, I also play an instrument. It's not the piano; it's the clarinet. But

I also learned about the impact that good practice has on results.

Personal references are a superb way of showing empathy. The person you refer to feels acknowledged and will smile at you. The entire audience perceives that you are spontaneous, kind and empathetic. That's exactly the perception you want to create.

You can refer to other people as well — technicians, organizers, cleaning staff, security personnel. What I like best is to refer to the other speakers, because that builds up your own ethos starting from their level — and they are, in a sense, your competitors on the stage. It shows that you are the least egocentric speaker at the event.

Boost your content even more by making references to the other speakers.

START A DIALOG

Interaction always has an impact — and the greatest impact comes when you start a one-to-one dialog with someone in your audience.

In 2010 I gave a TEDx talk on my European-spirit project in Barcelona. At one point I "attacked" this poor guy who was sitting in the third row. I had pictures of celebrity supporters up on the wall; I said to him:

I know what you're thinking. You — I know what you're thinking — "And where is U2?" [7]

Dialogs are great because they come across as totally natural. Just like being in the bar on a Saturday night at 11:30, talking to a friend. Imagine

---

[7] You can watch it in Spanish - with English subtitles — at bit.ly/tedxflorian — at minute 10:06.

a colleague of yours sitting in the audience — you look at him, make a hand gesture in his direction, and say:

Morten, you were right about what you said. When I hear all our fellow players in this market, it really looks like this sector is going to skyrocket.

Talking to one person in your audience has a strange but very real effect: the entire audience — as a unit — feels included in the conversation.

Include one-to-one dialogs in your talks. Your audiences will love them.

Boost your content even more by starting one-on-one dialogs with individuals in your audience.

CONTENT BRAKES

PLUSPLUS PATTERNS THAT IMPROVE YOUR SPEECHES AND
PRESENTATIONS EVERY TIME YOU AVOID THEM

THE SUSPENSE FREEZER

You start your speech. You unleash your first powerful paragraph; you state your key message, the objective of your talk, and — if necessary — you welcome the authorities and thank the organizers. That is the moment when most speakers present their agenda:

Today, I will talk about this and this and that.

Presenting an agenda at the beginning of a speech or presentation will always freeze the level of suspense down to the temperature of your fridge. Imagine a Hollywood movie in which they tell you at the beginning who will be killed, who will fall in love with whom, and how the hero saves the world.

No way! You don't *want* to know. Suspense and anticipation are vital in movies — and they are vital in speeches, too.

What I do in speeches, based on the Speech Structure Building™, is to mention my agenda at the end of the introduction, but without being specific about the content. My friend Conor calls it the sign-post.

I will share three powerful insights with you. The first one has to do with ...

If you do it this way, your audience knows that there will be three blocks of content, but they'll have to pay attention throughout the entire speech to find out what they are.

Even more creative is an agenda that presents an enigma. In my workshops on vocal variety I say, *I will talk about the three Cs of a great voice in public speaking. The first C has something to do with a vicious circle. The second C goes back to Voltaire. And the third C is... nothing!*

Don't be a suspense freezer — be a Hollywood screenplay writer.

Release the content brakes and don't use a dead fish agenda.

THE PAUSE KILLERS

Sioux Bean is a former member of Prestigious Speakers, my beloved Toastmasters club in Barcelona.

I was a rookie at our club, and Sioux fascinated me. I knew she was an English teacher from New Zealand. Being a native-speaker, she had an advantage over me, but still —

Sioux didn't use any filler sounds in her speeches. No *um*, no *ah*. Sioux didn't use any filler words, either. No *and, so, but, well, actually.*

Of all my friends from Toastmasters, it was Sioux who most inspired me. The way she used pauses made such a difference, compared to all the other speakers; the flow of her speeches was amazing.

Every *um*, every *ah, and, but, so, well* — is a pause killer. Filler words and filler sounds kill those wonderful, expressive pauses.

Once a seminar participant started her speech with a great polemic phrase followed by an even greater dramatic pause:

I'm sorry — 3-second pause! — I cannot tell you only good stories about my life.

Now imagine the same phrase with a pause killer:

I'm sorry, but ah, um, well, actually, I cannot tell you only good stories about my life.

Pauses are vital; they create suspense and drama in your speech. Please, please, please eliminate those pause killers!

Release the content brakes and kill the pause killers.

3.6 YEARS

When my son Álvaro was five years old, I bought him a dinosaur book. Like so many kids, he loves the T-Rex, and like so many parents, I also read those books with great interest. One number made me shiver.

Dinosaurs became extinct some 65 million years ago. I knew that. But did you know how many years dinosaurs populated this planet?

165,000,000 years.

Once I was reading Mark Twain's classic *Letters from the Earth,* and found another number that made me think a lot. When we look at the sky at night, we see bazillions of stars — 300 sextillion (more or less) by the latest estimates. But light takes time to travel. If we could travel at light speed, 299,792,458 meters per second, it would take 3.6 years to reach the solar system that's closest to us.

Aren't we small?

So there is absolutely no need at all to make ourselves even smaller — but that's exactly what we do all the time, both in everyday communication and on stage.

99% of all business presentations in Spain start like this:

Hoy vamos a hablar un poco de nuestra empresa.

Today we're going to talk a little bit about our company. Hey! Wait just a minute — what do you mean, *A little bit? ¡¿¡A little bit ?!?*

Your company is your passion, your life, your future — why would you want to talk about it *a little bit?*

I refer to things like this as "message reducers", and our vocabulary simply teems with them.

A little bit	little	small	short	simple
simply	quick	quickly	hopefully	probably
potentially	basically	actually	perhaps	maybe
could	should	would	ought to	think
believe	guess	try	want	pretty much
kind of	sort of	rather	quite	...

The list goes on — and on — and on. We are all world champions when it comes to diminishing our message — and ourselves.

Stop it!

You don't want to inflate yourself and get all puffed up. That would be perceived, justifiably, as arrogant. But, my friend, you don't want to make yourself smaller, either.

TURN THESE POORER PHRASES:

1. We're trying to achieve this goal.

2. I believe you can do it.

3. It's just an initiative.

4. We should be more aggressive in marketing and sales.

5. I will tell you a little bit about our company.

INTO THESE RICHER PHRASES:

1. We will achieve this goal!

2. I know you can do this!

3. It's a fantastic initiative!

4. Let's be more aggressive in marketing and sales!

5. I will share with you some exciting insights about our company!

Release the content brakes and throw out those message reducers.

ARE YOU AN AFFIRMATION SEEKER?

The British do it all the time.

It's a decent golf course, isn't it?

Isn't it? Don't we? Are we not?

The British are allowed to use this form of affirmation-seeking because they are smart people. The British use it as a rhetorical question.

However, it's a horse of a different color to make a statement, but then append one of the following diminutives:

We have accomplished great results this year — right?

This is how we'll do it, OK?

We have a great national team, eh?

To say "OK" is not OK. This is affirmation and approval seeking that does nothing but transmit uncertainty, which is pure poison for your ethos, your authoritativeness. Charismatic communicators make waterproof statements; they don't seek confirmation; they don't need it.

Release the content brakes and stop asking for affirmation.

DON'T TELL ME WHAT YOU'LL TELL ME

My friend Trent explained to me once that good American writing requires the elimination of all unnecessary content. Good writing is free of redundancies. So is good public speaking.

One pattern of redundant content is to introduce a story by saying that one will tell a story. There is no value in introductory phrases like...

I will tell you a little anecdote.

Let me tell you a story.

Let me tell you a joke.

A classic way to destroy dramatic tension is this:

Before I begin with my presentation, let me tell you a little story. At the age of ten, I dreamed of becoming a music star. I listened to Michael Jackson songs over and over again. ...

You've already learned that there is no such thing as a *little* story. But apart from this message reducer, can someone explain to me the reason for adding the first sentence?

At the age of ten, I dreamed of becoming a music star. I listened to Michael Jackson songs over and over again. ...

Imagine a grandmother, at dawn, sitting on the edge of her five-year old granddaughter's bed, saying,

Now I will tell you a fairytale. Once upon a time ...

No, she won't. She will simply start by saying,

Once upon a time...

Don't tell me what you're going to tell me. Just tell it!

Release the content brakes and take out redundant phrases.

BACKING AND FORTHING

I will get back to this on slide 18.

As I mentioned before, ...

I will refer to this point again later.

When you jump around in your content, you ask your audience to make mental jumps. Mental jumps are not good because they distract your audience from the flow of your argument. If you avoid them, nothing bad will happen. When you do get to slide 18, no one will remember that you referred to it before — or even worse, they're ignoring what you're saying while they wait for slide 18!

You take even bigger jumps when you say phrases like:

Let me get back to what I stated before.

Jumping around in your speech structure jeopardizes the logical flow of arguments. Instead, follow the logic of your Speech Structure Building™ and avoid jumping around.

Release the content brakes and avoid backing and forthing in your speech structure.

19 YEARS AGO

Every time speakers in my seminars mention dates like...

1993

Summer of 1989

October 1978

During Christmas 2005

I automatically start to do mental arithmetic, to figure out where I was at that time. Was I still in school? Wasn't that the year I took my final exams? Wasn't that the summer I fell in love for the first time, with Monica Vertes from Budapest?

Years and dates generate this mental process of personal reflection in your audience — and they can't do anything about it.

Just like backing and forthing around, this creates a mental distraction. We, as speakers, don't want mentally distracted audiences. We want to keep their attention fixed on what we're saying.

But there's a trick. You say exactly the same thing, but package it differently. You say:

19 years ago

23 years ago, during the summer

34 years ago, in the month of October

At Christmas, seven years ago

When we use periods of time, people in the audience don't start trying to calculate where they were back then. It would take an extra step of calculation, and most people just won't bother.

My tip is to replace all dates in the past and in the future with periods of time — weeks or months or years.

Release the content brakes and turn your dates into periods of time.

YOU ARE NOT LOUIS XIV

Some speakers love to talk about themselves in third person singular.

There was this little boy who weighed 30 kilograms too much.

That man has made mistakes in his life.

As a teenage girl, she was unhappy.

In the speech evaluation rounds I always remark that only Louis XIV and Julius Cesar were allowed to refer to themselves in the third person singular. All the rest of us mortal humans are wiser to avoid it.

Two reasons:

First, you can never fully get rid of the slightly arrogant tone.

Second, speaking in the third person is more impersonal; hence, it has less impact.

Speakers tend to use the third person when they bring up personal issues they feel uncomfortable about. Then they hide behind a schizoid wall of displacement.

But remember: the more personal you are, the more sincere you are. The more sincere you are, the better you connect with the audience.

Always make it personal:

When I was a little boy, I weighed 30 kilograms too much.

I've made mistakes in my life.

As a teenage girl, I was unhappy.

Release the content brakes and stop talking about yourself in the third person.

TWO DEMONS

Once, in the breakfast room of a hotel, I met a guy who was supposed to participate in my seminar that day. Chewing on my hard-boiled egg, I asked him his name. In German he answered:

Stephan.

I asked, *Stephan written with "ph" or with an "f"?*

With a "k".

His sarcastic comment was followed by a loud, exaggerated, scornful sounding laugh.

Sarcasm and cynicism are two demons of public speaking. Sarcasm is critical; cynicism is bitter. Like the demons in stories, if you let them loose, they are most likely to turn against you. Using either will reveal to your audience feelings that you probably would prefer to keep to yourself: feelings of hurt and anger that you have not yet resolved. Up on stage before an audience is not the time or place to engage in working through negative feelings; save that for private moments with a spouse, a friend, or a therapist. Don't talk about it in public until you can do so in a positive way.

Release the content brakes and avoid being sarcastic or cynical.

MINEFIELDS OF ANTIPATHY

Women can't drive.

Chinese people eat dogs.

Socialists are corrupt.

Who needs religion?

Vegetarians are strange people.

Sexism, racism, politics, religion — all the above statements plant dangerous cluster-bombs in the minefields of antipathy.

The above lines are obvious landmines, but there are other statements we sometimes make — without any bad intentions — that can cause equal harm to your position as a speaker.

Once a German man, speaking about his life, told how he'd made an important decision in his late teens; he'd decided to do one year of civil service instead of serving in the military.

No problem with that — in those days, when serving the country was still obligatory for every male citizen in Germany, about half followed the same path. But — he stepped onto a landmine of antipathy when he said why he made that choice: *I didn't want to shoot at people.*

In the evaluation round I asked the crowd: *Did any of you guys serve in the military?*

Three men raised their hands. I continued: *And did you like it when our friend here said that he didn't serve in the military because he didn't want to shoot at people?*

No, they said. All three of them.

You can give a brilliant twenty-minute talk, but make just one disparaging comment against smokers, and you lose 40% of your audience. Be very careful about what you say. Avoid the classical minefields of antipathy — sex, religion and politics — and also be cautious with your personal views. They could cost you a big portion of your audience unnecessarily.

Release the content brakes and avoid statements that are harmful to you because they disparage part of your audience.

S***!

*F***! S***! A******!*

I work a lot for the online sector. The online sector is full of vibes and vigor — young people with a vision, successful entrepreneurs in their twenties, geeks and hackers, venture capitalists and crazy guys.

People in the online sector speak a different language, a youthful argot that embraces a multitude of four-letter words.

When I criticize their use of four-letter words in the feedback rounds, they often say: *But everyone uses them. Didn't you say we should speak in the language of the people we're talking to?*

It's true. Speaking the language of your audience helps you connect with them. From Martin Luther King to Adolf Hitler, history is full of both terrific and terrifying examples.

However, to the contrary, four-letter words do not help you connect with your audience; rather, they drag your style down, your class, the level of your ethos as a leader. The funny thing about four-letter words is that no one misses them when you leave them out. No one will ever come up to you after your speech and say, *Hey, you didn't say "shit"!*

A sophisticated trick is to sprinkle your four-letter words into dialogs.

When he knew that our venture was going down, my partner said, "Oh, shit!"

You didn't say it — your partner did.

In general, I recommend that you eliminate four-letter words from the language you use to speak in public. Class and ethos count for much more than a short shock or a quick, cheap laugh.

Release the content brakes and skip the four-letter words.

NEVER SAY YOU'RE SORRY

It was a Toastmasters speech — I remember it so well. I gave a talk on my European project, facebook.com/thefestival. An experienced American woman from Munich took the role of evaluating my speech.

At one point, I had wanted to mention three European countries:

Poland, Slovakia and — and — and — oh, sorry, now I forgot the third country.

The speech went on smoothly. When it was her turn, the woman from the U.S. did a great job evaluating it. As usual, she mentioned several good points and why she liked them. Then she moved on to the PLUSPLUS side, and right away she homed in on that one unutterable word. She said: *Never ever, ever, ever say "Sorry" on stage! Excusing yourself kills your authority as a speaker.*

From that moment onward, I have never, ever, ever, ever again said "Sorry" on stage.

When I go blank on stage, I pause — for as long as it takes — but I don't say "Sorry"!

When I sneeze on stage, I continue as if nothing had happened.

When I drop a flipchart marker on stage, I pick it up and keep writing.

In your relationships, you're allowed to say, "Sorry"; sometimes you do need to say it. On stage, you're not allowed to, and you don't need to.

Release the content brakes and stop saying "Sorry".

THE GENERAL ASSUMPTION TRAP

Do you recall what Mark Twain said about generalizations? One of my absolute favorite PLUSPLUS patterns is the trap of making general assumptions. On stage and in everyday life, we frequently say:

Everyone likes...

We all know that...

We've all had this experience before...

All the time, people assume that everbody likes this or knows that. But — it's a trap!

Once, in a seminar, my client's CFO claimed:

We all love to go shopping.

In the evaluation round after that speech, the CEO raised his hand and barked:

I hate shopping!

There is no such thing as "everyone knows" or "everybody likes" something. Every time you fall into this trap and make a general assumption, you'll tread on the toes of several people in your audience. It's those people who'll make negative comments afterwards, during the coffee break.

The solution is simple. Instead of assuming, you ask:

Who likes to go shopping?

Who of you knows...?

Did you ever have the experience of...?

When you ask questions, you'll always be on the safe side. And you can build spontaneous bridges of sympathy with those who do raise their hands:

Those of you who love to go shopping — let me tell you this...

You've learned already that asking questions is a great way to interact with your audience. Asking questions is a positive, creative way to get around the trap of making general assumptions.

Release the content brakes and eschew general assumptions.

GOOSEBUMPS IN THE AIR

There are two paragraphs that you will learn by heart. Not only will you learn them by heart, but you will get them *right*. You will achieve *excellence* in your intonation, your diction, your pauses.

The two paragraphs in question are your first one, and your last. Those two paragraphs create the first and the final impressions that you make on your audience. Those two paragraphs have the most massive impact on whether you get an overall thumbs-up or thumbs-down. You cannot permit yourself to screw up.

You have learned about five ways to open your speech. Now let's take a look at your closing.

The vast majority of my seminar participants' first speeches end with the same phrase: *And that's it — thank you.*

And that's it, thank you — ??? Wow, how very exciting! This will blast your audience against the back wall of the room, from the excitement.

And that's it, thank you — ? How very persuasive, how very motivational, how very inspirational!

You can do better!

One great way to end a speech is to involve your audience with a question.

Example: "Heroes"

You have learned about the three heroes of my life. You have met my dad, who taught me my love for nature. You have met my best friend and partner Rose, who stood by my side during my dark times. You have met my son

*Álvaro, whose innocent smile can move mountains. Now ask yourselves —
who are the heroes in your life?*

Such a heroic topic might cause goosebumps in the audience. They
leave the room reflecting on the heroes in their own lives. You simply
cannot add a "Thank you" to such a closing.

But I have to say "Thank you" at the end, they protest.

Yeah, sure — if you're a dead fish floating downstream! But you don't
have to say "Thank you" just because everybody else does.

I never say *Thank you* at the end of a speech. And not once has someone
approached me during the coffee break afterwards and said to me, *Hey,
you didn't say "Thank you"!*

The gray mass is driven by gray standards. If you aim at being an even
better communicator, you need to add some color to your style.

For me, a "Thank you" kills the vibrations in the room that you built up
with the final lines of your speech. Imagine a closing like, *If we do not
act today, we will be gone by tomorrow. Thank you.*

No, Thanks!

Build a strong closing; raise goosebumps in the audience with last
sentences like, *I love you, Dad* — and skip that stupid "Thank you"!

**Release the content brakes and erase the words "Thank you" from
your closing.**

II. DELIVERY

DELIVERY BOOSTERS

PLUSPLUS PATTERNS THAT IMPROVE YOUR SPEECHES AND
PRESENTATIONS EVERY TIME YOU APPLY THEM

CHECKED

All good public speaking requires thorough preparation. On his blog mannerofspeaking.org, my friend and co-creator of "Rhetoric – The Public Speaking Game™" John Zimmer has published an extensive checklist for public speaking logisitics.

I recommend you download this list, which includes various categories, such as travel, communication, venue, equipment, marketing, consumables, and presentation.

John's checklist makes sure you don't miss out key preparatory steps, like meeting the host, meeting the technicians, preparing the speaking area, or having a spare shirt — just in case.

Once you've checked everything, you're ready for your appearance on stage. "Be Prepared" is the motto of the Boy Scouts; make it yours, too.

Boost your delivery even more by being thoroughly prepared for your performance.

TOO SHORT IS ALWAYS GOOD

Never has a speech been bad for being too short. It's always the other way around. That's why it's crucial to manage your time; it will make your public speaking even better.

Think about all the conference speeches you have experienced in the last five or ten years. How many of them went past their alloted time? And how many of them were just way too long?

I have competed in several Toastmasters International speech competitions. In these contests, speeches must be five to seven minutes long.

Since these were competitions, I would write out my speeches and learn them by heart, verbatim. It's quite possible to memorize a seven-minute speech.

I recommend that you always write out important speeches, whether you learn them by heart or not. It's good exercise, and you'll find that writing creates its own inspiration. Your rhetoric improves; you have time to find better words and more effective expressions, to eliminate verbosity, and to make your points clearly, directly, and succinctly.

I've prepared, rehearsed, and delivered several speeches in competition, and I've learned a useful pattern: if I use Arial 12 with 1.5-line spacing, then one DIN A4 page equals approximately three minutes.

Once I gave an inspirational speech at the Berlin-based online conference Heureka! The organizers had planned a 15-minute slot for me. I wrote the speech word by word, but only used four and a half pages (Arial 12, 1.5-line spacing). That, according to my experience, translated into 13½ minutes — and that was my exact intention.

Time management = speech length < slot time

Always prepare a speech or presentation that's shorter than the time you've been alloted to deliver it. The audience will love you. The event organizers will love you too, because you'll gain back some of the time your predecessors on the stage used up.

Boost your delivery even more by writing shorter speeches.

SHUT UP, WAIT, AND SMILE

When you walk into a hotel, what are your first impressions?

When you board a plane, what are your first impressions?

When you enter a restaurant, what are your first impressions?

According to businessdictionary.com, a "moment of truth" is an instance of contact or interaction between a customer and a firm (through a product, call, or visit) that gives the customer an opportunity to form (or change) an impression about the firm.

Moments of truth don't happen only in marketing and customer service. Moments of truth also exist in public speaking. Think of your audience as the customer, with yourself as the company. You want them to get the best first impression possible.

And your speech doesn't begin when you first start making verbal sounds. It starts even earlier than that.

Many speakers have already started talking while they're still walking out onto the stage. That is an absolute not-to-do! It's a complete brake on your delivery! You will *never* do this again in your entire life!

You need absolute silence in the room when you begin, and that silence depends on one person and one person only: *you.*

The first moment of truth is a moment of silence. You don't say *Well;* you don't say *Hello;* you don't say *Ah;* you don't clear your throat. You walk up on stage and shut up.

The second moment of truth is a moment of patience. Shutting up alone isn't enough to make your audience stop squeaking their chairs, coughing like horses, or playing with their smart phones. That requires patience. Look at them, and wait. Don't begin to speak until there is absolute silence in the room.

The third moment of truth is the moment of a smile. While you're shutting up and being patient, you smile at your audience. You smile the kind of smile that made my dad the happiest man on earth.

What you accomplish with these three moments of truth is the perception of absolute authority combined with self-confidence. PLUS, you have 100% of their attention.

Boost your delivery even more by employing the three moments of truth.

THE LINE OF PROXIMITY

My mother was an elementary school teacher for more than 40 years, and her total pedagogical experience spans 56 years. My mother knows education.

We were in Bamberg, Bavaria, at Schlenkerla, where the waitresses have been buxom and the beer has tasted like smoked ham since before 1405. As we were enjoying a heavy lunch, she told me the story of the zebra with the horizontal stripes.

It was her personal psychological experiment. When she had a new class of first graders, early on she would carefully draw six zebras on the chalkboard. Five of them would have vertical stripes; one of them would have horizontal stripes.

Then she would turn to her class and ask: *So — which one is the evil zebra?*

Without a millisecond of thought, and all in unison, they would scream as loud as they could, together in a despiteous voice: *That one, that one!*

Sometimes it's not the news media telling you who is good and who is evil. Sometimes it's not your professor, nor your parents, nor your friends. Sometimes it's your own cerebellum — you're assailed by the voice of your instincts before you even have a chance to switch on your power to reason.

The evil one must be the one that's different from the rest. You can cheat your reason, but you can't cheat your instincts. And the challenge you face in public speaking is: *you* are the zebra with horizontal stripes.

Everyone in your audience has vertical stripes. They form a unit. You are the stranger, the outsider, the one no one really trusts. Knowing this, it's crucial for you, as a public speaker, to build bridges of trust with your audience. One of these bridges of trust is respecting the line of proximity.

Too much physical distance from your audience transmits a subconscious message of fear. But being too close transmits a subconscious message of intimidation. Just the right distancing transmits a subconscious message of self-confidence and trust.

So the line of proximity is the least possible distance between you and your audience — without being intimidating, and without showing your back to any of your audience. Before you speak, define for yourself that mental line of proximity, according to the way the room is set up, and the way it feels. Trust your feelings. And as always, preparation is everything.

When you stand on the line of proximity, your audience will still see you as that zebra with horizontal stripes. But they'll trust you more and like you better. And the best part of it is, they won't know why.

Boost your delivery even more by positioning yourself on the line of proximity.

YOU ARE NOT A TIN SOLDIER

When you were a kid, did you play with tin soldiers? I did — the Prussian army against Napoleon Bonaparte. It was great fun for a while — but then it started to get boring. My tin soldiers were too monotonous, too stiff. They didn't move.

On stage many speakers are tin soldiers. They're stiff. They seem stuck in one place, and they don't move at all. They hold their position, and the audience thinks, *Hey, that's just like a tin soldier!*

But you're not. You can easily boost the impact of your speech delivery by moving around on stage instead of standing stiff and still, as if you're protecting yourself. A confident speaker takes command of the stage.

Are you a skier? Have you ever skied? If so, then you know that your chest should always be facing toward the valley, the downhill slope. My recommendation is that you move along the line of proximity like a crawfish — left to right, right to left, remembering always to keep your chest facing downhill, toward the valley!

Moving horizontally on stage transmits calmness, confidence, leadership, and authority. And it definitely shows that you're not a tin soldier.

Boost your delivery even more by showing that you can move.

MOVE, STAND, AND SPEAK

Some people in your audience want to see you stand; others want to see you move. A good way to please both groups is to move, then take your stance, then speak.

As an example: You learned above about the content boosting effect of the Speech Structure Building™. Comprising that building, there's the opening (the foundation), the three pillars (A – B – C), and the closing (the roof).

Now — imagine you're speaking about the evolution of Velcro.

You position yourself in the center of your stage, touching the line of proximity, and you start speaking.

It was an accident. A man had gone hunting. The seed of a blowball flew through the air and got stuck on his woolen clothes. That man had an idea. One of the greatest success stories of intellectual property in modern history began during a casual walk through the mountains. The idea for Velcro was born. What happened next?

Now you move to the right side of the stage (from your point of view). You take your stance and continue to speak.

Ever since then, Velcro has moved in only one direction: success, success, success. It all started with the first contract —

What is the role of Velcro today?

Then move to the center of the stage and continue.

Today Velcro has penetrated literally all sectors and product types. Velcro is vital in the automotive industry; Velcro is essential in the shoe industry;

Velcro is fundamental in the clothing industry —

And where do we see Velcro in the future?

Move to the left side of the stage (again, from your point of view). You take your stance and continue to speak.

No one can see the future. But the future sees Velcro …

Finally, you move back to the central position.

Mr. Oogway, the wise turtle in Kung Fu Panda, just like Picasso, once said: "There are no accidents." Velcro had to happen. One of the most successful inventions in the last 100 years has found its past, its present and its future. Maybe it was no accident at all.

You don't have to follow such a strict path of stage movements, but your audience will always appreciate it (again, without realizing why) when you enhance your content transitions with a step to the left or a step to the right.

Finally, whenever you convey a key message or an important fact, whenever you add a dramatic pause or other elements that build drama — stop moving, take your stance — then speak.

Boost your delivery even more by moving, standing, then speaking.

THE PRINCESS LEIA EFFECT

Star Wars! I was nine years old when I saw R2D2 delivering the message from Princess Leia for the first time. I was totally thrilled by Hollywood's first holographic transmission.

On stage you can also use holograms. I call it the Princess Leia effect. What's different from R2D2's visual transmission is that on stage you create *imaginary* images in the minds of your audience.

Once I started my class at IESE Busines School in Barcelona in a different way. I didn't use a quotation. I didn't use a polemic phrase. I didn't use one portentous word, nor a question, nor a personal anecdote.

Instead, I held my right hand out in front of myself, at head-height, palm up, fingers spread. For a good while I stared at what was sitting on the palm of my hand — which was nothing.

120 eyes, 60 brilliant and smart Executive MBAs, were staring with me — at nothing!

Then, after a while, I turned my hand into a fist and exclaimed: *You've already learned your first lesson: You were looking at nothing!*

My friend, staging expert Jerzy Zientkowski, says, *The power of holograms on stage is amazing. You can paint an endless number of objects in the minds of your audience.* To be a holographic Picasso, you need well-controlled body language, hand gestures, and facial expressions.

Here are some examples:

You point with your finger at a spot some metres away, to your right. You look at that spot and say: *That piano in the corner of our living room —*

Or you turn your head 135° to your right and extend your arm out in the same direction; you open your fingers as if you were touching something. Then you say: *My friend Sven, who was sitting in the back of the car, looked tired.*

You hold out your hands, palms down, and move them so as to describe a rectangle about the size of a briefcase. While you're doing this, you say: *The symbol of my perseverance is a big old grayish Samsonite suitcase.*

When I painted that Samsonite suitcase in the minds of my audience during an inspirational speech in Berlin, 550 people were able to see it.

They'll see Samsonite suitcases; they'll see pianos; they'll see friends in the back seat of the car. And since visual images are always more powerful than words, you'll increase the impact of your speech tremendously.

Boost your delivery even more by creating holographic images in the minds of your audience — R2D2-style.

HANDS UP!

What should I do with my hands?

Do you know how many times I've heard this question? I don't — I've stopped counting.

Now that you know about the Princess Leia effect, you already have an idea. Good hand gestures are extremely important in public speaking. They emphasize your content. They make your message more memorable. They underline your enthusiasm. And without good hand gestures, you can never create holograms on stage. Don't ever underestimate the power of the Princess Leia effect.

In "Rhetoric – The Public Speaking Game™" we created one challenge card that says: Keep your hands tight at your side and tell an exciting story. Even the great John Zimmer had to slightly move his fingers. You learn most about the power of your hands when suddenly you cannot use them.

So then — what should you do with your hands?

Move them! Paint pictures! Do sign language!

When you speak about opening an egg, open the egg with your hands.

When you speak about Spanish red wine, have a sip from the glass in your right or left hand.

When you speak about your child, indicate his or her height with one hand.

Gottfried, a fabulous chef from Munich who collects Asian art, represented the "rabbit party" in one of my seminars on charisma. In his final campaign speech, he held his hands up beside his head and shouted:

Our ears are always attuned to society's problems!

Boost your delivery even more by using hand gestures.

PROP UP YOUR SPEECH

I could say: *I'm German.*

Or I could hold up my German passport and say: *I'm German.*

Props, visual aids, are an indispensable tool for any public speaker. They make your message more tangible, more understandable, more memorable.

Here are three examples of different sorts of props. They're extreme, but that's because I mean to inspire you to become more creative and to plan, every time you speak, to include 3d objects.

A FUN PROP

I'm from Bavaria, and I love beer. I will never hide my passion for it. Once I decided to devote a speech to my love for the malt and hops.

The first sentence was not a first sentence at all. Instead, I opened a bottle of beer, smiled at my audience, poured the beer into a glass, and drank it all down in a single draught. Then — after a pause — I said, *I love beer!*

This might not be an appropriate move in a professional business presentation. Or then again, maybe it might.

Imagine you are a fraud-detection specialist, and you give a talk to a number of French prospects. You hold a glass of red wine in your hand, take a sip, and say, *In vino veritas. — The Romans knew it; we know it. Our business is the truth.*

Why not? French people love red wine. They might appreciate an opening like that.

Sure, it always depends on your audience. But my experience is that the reward for doing something different in public speaking always makes me feel glad that I was able to override my fear of doing something wrong.

AN INTERACTIVE PROP

When you are the moderator at a Toastmasters[8] meeting, it's great to come up with a topic for the session. I've seen a vast variety of themes throughout the years, including the Olympic Games, quotations, Christmas, the fall of the Iron Curtain, and the three little pigs.

In one club meeting I chose secrets as the leitmotif. I wanted some of my fellow club members to reveal unknown facets of their lives. So, to give that concept a good push, I distributed some raw red beans, one to each of the members and the guests, before the meeting.

When I took the stage, I asked the group, *Please throw those beans at me.*

Some of them threw those beans as hard as they could. I could feel the dark side, the Mr. Hyde within several of my friends. When the painful shower ended, I smiled at them and said, *You've just spilled the beans.*

Spilling the beans built the bridge to the theme of the evening — sharing secrets.

Interactive props are great; audiences love them. But again, do make sure you adapt your interactive idea to your specific audience.

A DRAMATIC PROP

On another occasion I gave a dramatic talk. The speech was about a trip to New York that ended tragically.

---

8 Haven't you checked toastmasters.org yet?

At one point in the story I yelled at this one guy and slammed some coins down at his feet. Right at that moment, I reached into my pocket, took out a few real coins, and smashed them down on the floor in front of my shocked audience.

Whether you use a glass of beer, raw red beans, coins, newspapers or books, a piece of granite, or a diving outfit — keep the following three points in mind:

Props must always:

    1) be unique,

    2) support, enhance and illustrate your message, and

    3) have a surprise effect.

Boost your delivery even more by making your message more memorable with props.

SMILE, SMILE, SMILE

I've seen so many of them — the happiest people, the funniest guys, the joke tellers. Always in a good mood, always loud, always shining until —

It's amazing to see what happens to people when they step into the spotlight. In one millisecond their facial expression switches from sunhine to rain, from wedding to funeral, from *Mary Poppins* to *Nightmare On Elm Street*.

Where does their smile go?

Without your smile you are nothing. No smile, no enthusiasm; no enthusiasm, no moving an audience to action. Your smile transmits so much on stage: self-confidence, passion, enthusiasm, positivity, optimism.

You need to smile on stage! Smile before you start to speak; smile when you've finished, and if it fits your tone and content, smile throughout, too.

Smile even when it's over — and even if it's difficult. My friend Olivia Schofield made it to the final nine of the World Championship of Public Speaking in 2011. She gave a superbly inspirational speech about overcoming her speech impediment. Many of the more than 2000 attendees thought she was going to make it to the podium.

Olivia went 15 seconds overtime and was disqualified. But as she was standing there on stage, she took it with a smile. She knew she'd given it her best — and she knew everyone was watching her. Olivia is one of my greatest heroes on stage! Olivia smiled.

Boost your delivery even more by smiling.

A SPRINGBOARD OF AUTHENTICITY

I was thirteen years old when my parents got divorced.

This is what one seminar participant revealed once, during a speech. But while he was saying it, he was smiling — awkwardly, but smiling.

I could see it coming: during the evaluation one of his fellow attendees expressed her feeling that there was no coherence between his content and his facial expression when he mentioned the divorce. It did not feel authentic to her.

Frankly, would you smile while talking about your parents' divorce, which caused your life to take an agonizing turn right when you were at the peak of puberty?

"To cohere" is to hold or stick together. According to Merriam-Webster, "coherence" is the quality or state of cohering, as a) systematic or logical connection or consistency, or b) integration of diverse elements, relationships, or values.

The triangle of coherence: of body, voice, and content, directly influences your level of authenticity as the audience perceives it. Therefore, the triangle of coherence needs to be in a state of balance in public speaking.

As a public speaker you face a multi-dimensional matrix of permutations and combinations (see below). It takes time, practice and feedback to find that state of balance in any speaking situation.

Body: Facial expressions, hand and arm gestures, legs, entire body

Voice: Loud, soft, fast, slow, pitch, pause

Content: Technical, entertaining, emotional, inspirational

Despite the time, practice and feedback it takes to become a master of coherence, there are some common-sense ideas you can easily apply right from the start.

For instance, when you speak about your parents' divorce, your smile will disappear. Instead, you'll look sad. Your voice gets quieter. You pause repeatedly, which communicates your hesitancy to speak. You avoid the all-important eye contact for a moment and look at the floor instead, which expresses your embarrassment. You speak slowly and thoughtfully. Your hands hang low. Now your triangle of coherence is in balance.

When you speak about your experience with hurricane Sandy, your voice gets louder. Your pitch gets a little higher. You speak more rapidly — your vowels stumble across your consonants. Your hands and arms flail around. A terrified gaze — panic in your eyes — the hurricane is coming! Now your triangle of coherence is in balance.

When you speak about the objectives you want your sales team to accomplish, your voice will be loud, firm, and determined. You'll make dramatic pauses after each motivational statement. You'll look deeply into people's eyes with self-confidence and authority. You'll clench your fist like Rafael Nadal after he's made his match point. Now your triangle of coherence is in balance.

In a 1985 interview, at a time when his teeth still needed work, my super hero Jim Carrey said, *My best friend is the mirror*. You can practice your coherence in public speaking every day and almost everywhere — in front of mirrors at home, in hotels, in bathrooms — almost anywhere. Coherence is not about being an actor. It's about expressing yourself in an authentic way. If you do that, then certainly you'll never smile again when you talk about your parents' divorce.

Boost your delivery even more practicing coherence of body, voice and content.

THE NOD

There is another crucial form of coherence — the coherence between content and eye contact.

Imagine you're holding up a photo of a Central African child soldier. You speak about the agony this little eight-year-old boy has gone through: drugged, sexually abused, given alcohol, forced to kill innocent people.

Isn't it horrible?

While you say it, you do not look at that 16-year old skateboarder on the left side of the front row.

No — it's better if you look at that lady in her mid-forties in the middle of the fourth row. She might have children eight or ten years old.

You look that lady deeply into her eyes while you ask that rhetorical question:

Isn't it horrible?

And she will do what you're looking for her to do. She will nod.

That nod is what we live for as public speakers — the nod of affirmation. When that lady nods, confirming what you said, a domino effect of empathy ripples through the rows.

Analyze your audience before you walk on stage. At those key points during your speech, make sure you look at the right people. Hunt for that nod!

Boost your delivery even more by looking at the right people at the right moment.

THE MOST EFFECTIVE WORD

The ubiquitous Mark Twain said: *No word was ever as effective as a rightly timed pause.* I couldn't agree more. All great speeches include pauses — without pauses, no speech can be great.

Pauses give you three benefits:

First, when you pause, you gain some time to think about what you're planning to say — (pause) — two seconds later.

Second, when you pause, you gain time to — (pause) — breathe. Deep, purposeful breathing is essential for good vocal volume and variety. Use the time of a pause to take a deep breath. It also helps you to relax.

Third, when you pause, you add — (pause) — drama to your speech.

Examples:

And you know what I did then? — (long pause) — Nothing.

I committed the biggest mistake of my life — (longer pause) — I fired my friend.

The happiest moment of my life came — (longest pause) — when I held my son in my arms for the very first time.

The interesting thing about pauses is — that there are two worlds of perception: yours as the speaker, and the audience's. On stage, you'll feel as if a three-second pause lasts two hours, but your audience experiences a three-second pause and appreciates each additional moment even more.

I learned that a pause can never be too long. Once, during a speech competition, I went blank at the beginning, shortly after the opening. I suffered for more or less eight seconds, till I finally got back on track. I won the competition. They hadn't even noticed that I'd had a problem. They'd thought I was pausing for dramatic effect. There is no such thing as too long a pause.

Boost your delivery even more by adding pauses.

YOUR VOICE IS A ROLLERCOASTER

It took Pedro from Barcelona five minutes — they were the longest five minutes of his life.

With great anticipation we were sitting in the seminar room. Eight people. Eyes closed. We could hear Pedro's coughing. We could feel his gulping sounds when he sipped from his water bottle.

Then silence. First a silence of desperation, then a silence of resignation.

Would he really do it now?

Another cough, another sip, another silence.

Then suddenly the vulcano erupted.

GOOOOOOOOOOOOOOOOOOOOOOOOOOOOOOOOL

We rose to our feet. We cheered! We clapped! We jumped up and swarmed around Pedro and gave him a big hug!

Pedro had just celebrated an imaginary goal by his favorite football team, F.C. Barcelona. His voice was so loud that people from the neighboring room held up purple balloons painted with angry faces. We could see them through the window on top of the wall.

But Pedro didn't care. He was smiling from ear to ear. For the first time in his life he'd used his voice in an authentic way in front of other people. He felt relieved — but more, he felt exhilarated.

Your voice is a rollercoaster. You can speak in a loud tone; you can speak in a soft tone. You can speak slowly, or you can speak rapidly. And when the rollercoaster is about to go down the starting ramp, you don't speak at all. You — pause.

Whether it's in a football stadium, at a funeral, at a wedding, during a nasty fight with a friend, a passionate discussion with an Italian taxi driver, tender talk after sex, a touching declaration of love, a crazy night in the pub in Dublin with Boris, Tiho, Christoph, and Yves — you already know your voice, and it's ready!

You use your voice all the time. Do the same on stage, and shout "GOL!" like at Camp Nou. Then you will project your authenticity!

Boost your delivery even more by using your voice on stage as you do in normal life.

THE BIGGEST DIFFERENCE

Nothing great was ever achieved without enthusiasm.

— Ralph Waldo Emerson

When my friend Olivia Schofield and I both arrived early at a public speaking conference in Poznan, Poland, we got to talking about what makes the difference in public speaking. What distinguishes a great speaker from the huge mass of merely good and adequate speakers?

We agreed on one element: energy.

It's your energy and enthusiasm that drive your delivery. Imagine Martin Luther King giving his "I have a dream" speech in a dull, boring, monotonous tone. No volume to his voice, no variety, no — pauses. No intonation. No energy. No enthusiasm.

Would his speech have inspired thousands upon thousands in front of the Lincoln Memorial? Would the video of his speech have received so many millions of views on YouTube?

We know that he had practiced in small chapels in Alabama, Georgia and Mississippi — thousands of times.

They say: *But he was a preacher.*

I say: *Then be a preacher!*

Your voice is one of the tools you use to express your enthusiasm and energy on stage. Your body is the other. At the Lincoln Memorial, Martin Luther King was standing behind a lectern. Imagine him on a larger stage with a headset and with no walls between him and the audience. Wow — that would have been even more powerful.

Energy (Enthusiasm) = Voice + Body

Your body whispers; your body speaks; your body shouts, and your body screams.

Make your body talk when you feel small and insignificant.

Make your body talk when you wave good-bye to your loved ones before boarding a plane.

Make your body talk when you speak about dancing the tango.

Make your body talk when you say that you're a fanatic golfer.

Make your body talk when you're fed up with something.

The biggest difference between a great speaker and a merely adequate speaker is energy. Your body and your voice make all the difference. Always use them much, much more than you think you can, or should.

Boost your delivery even more by pumping up your energy and enthusiasm.

THE QUEEN OF DRAMA

Are you familiar with the Gaussian function, also called the bell curve? Carl Friedrich Gauss, the German mathematician and physical scientist, used this curve to describe the normal distribution, which now is the most basic tool of statistical analysis.

We tend to belive that our entire audience approves or disapproves of the way we're communicating. But in any given speech, the perception of your audience will follow that same bell curve: 5 to 10% of every crowd will think you're an idiot, and another 5 to 10% will think you're a genius. The reactions of the rest will fall somewhere in-between, just as predicted by the bell curve.

Your principal objective as a public speaker is to win the approval of more than half the audience.

Bill Cosby once said: *I don't know the key to success, but the key to failure is trying to please everybody.*

You'll never please 100% of your audience, but it also would be a misconception to believe that all of them disapprove of you, or think you're being ridiculous. When I give seminars to eight people, I always say that we have nine different points of view in the room.

For most people, acting is a torture chamber of feeling ridiculous — especially in front of groups of people. It comes from being self-conscious. On the other hand, I know, from having seen thousands of speeches, that drama can spice up your delivery enormously.

You've already learned how valuable dialogs can be for the content of your speeches. Whether you're an actor or not, dialogs turn you into one.

When you recount dialogs you've had with clients, colleagues, bosses or friends, your entire attitude changes. Your voice changes; your facial expressions change; even your body language changes.

I learned a good tip from Peter Zinn, my Dutch storytelling friend. When you recount a dialog with another character (who's not actually there), don't move from one side to another on stage. Instead, turn your body 90° from half left to half right, back and forth. You can take advantage of the Princess Leia effect. It's effective; it looks smooth, and it's not so strenuous.

The very same Olivia Schofield is my queen of drama. She is a trained actress and dancer who became a pro at public speaking. She admits that it's two different worlds. But she also acknowledges the advantages she enjoys from using certain acting techniques in her speeches. I've seen her in action, and I guarantee you: Olivia makes an impact!

When you add drama to your speech you will lose that 5 to 10% of your audience that gets turned off by it. But really, who cares? Think about the Gaussian function; some people will always make negative comments about your speech; some people are always looking for negative things to say — they will never learn the secret of PLUSPLUS. But when you add drama to your speeches, what's certain is that you won't be the dead fish passively floating with the flow.

Boost your delivery even more by adding drama.

DO IT YOUR WAY

When you act on stage while speaking in public, you'll lose 5 or 10% of your audience. And you can take off another 5 or 10% when you sing. I'm a great fan of singing Sinatra's "My Way", so I have to admit that I'm biased when it comes to singing during a speech.

When I sing in my seminar speeches, I almost always hear one PLUS-PLUS comment by a participant. I told you — 5 to 10%.

But — what about the other 90 to 95% of your audience?

In that same TEDx talk about Europe, in which I did that one-to-one dialog (see "Start A Dialog", above), I started the presentation by performing our European hip-hop song.[9] Not possible?

---

9 www.bit.ly/tedxflorian

You cannot sing in a business presentation!

Have you ever tried?

No.

So how can you say that you cannot sing during a business presentation?

It's always the same. I've talked about it so many times! But people won't believe it until they try it — and receive positive feedback for it. Take Stefan for example.

Stefan, a revenue manager for a four-star hotel, presented his life in one of my seminars. Along the way he mentioned that, as a kid, he had performed the role of one of the three boys in Mozart's *Magic Flute*. He added casually that they went on a world tour, and that the highlight was a series of six perfomances in Tel Aviv.

As always, after his talk I moderated a positive and constructive evaluation of Stefan's speech. It went normally until, at one point, I stopped, looked at him and asked:

You did what? I want to hear you sing — now!

I still see the shock in Stefan's eyes. And what was Pedro's F.C. Barcelona (see "Your Voice Is A Rollercoaster", above) became Stefan's *Magic Flute.*

It took us about eight minutes. More covered eyes, more coughing, more gulping — but he did it. In a tenor voice, Stefan raised more goosebumps in that room than the movie *Titanic* could ever have done. It was wonderful. The exuberant applause took Stefan by surprise, and his self-esteem got a huge shot in the arm.

In a follow-up seminar on charisma six months later, Stefan was speaking about his strengths. He underlined his love for music by singing a sequence from another musical piece by Mozart. Without our having to cover our eyes, and with his own humble self-confidence, Stefan won our hearts. His charisma level exploded like a volcano.

The number one excuse is: I can't sing. It's funny, but to this day I've never seen a single speaker receive the constructive feedback of being advised to refrain from singing. Whatever the sort of voice, the feedback has always been on the PLUS side.

Don't be a dead fish! Swim against the flow! Singing is a great boost to your delivery. It will win you the approval of a large portion of your audience. Do it your way!

Boost your delivery even more with singing.

DELIVERY BRAKES

PLUSPLUS PATTERNS THAT IMPROVE YOUR SPEECHES AND PRESENTATIONS EVERY TIME YOU AVOID THEM

THEY ARE LIKE EARMUFFS

This is one of my favorite passages from my first book, *The Seven Minute Star:*

The use of notes in public speaking is like earmuffs. You can wear them, but they will never look good on you.

So, one thing about them is the poor appearance you have when you hold notes in your hand. But it's not only that.

What's even more significant is that you cut off your nonverbal communication when you use notes. How can you take advantage of the Princess Leia effect when you hold a bunch of papers in your left hand? How can you create a vision evoking your passion for cooking when you hold a bunch of papers in your right hand? How can you perform any hand gestures at all — with a bunch of papers in your hand?

The third and most important reason to avoid using notes has to do with your level of ethos. What you do when you speak in public — at least in a business environment — is sell ideas, products, and services. You sell your company, you sell your strategy, you sell — yourself. When you speak in public, you're selling.

Now, wouldn't you agree that creating the impression of knowledge and expertise is vital to generating the credibility you must convey as a salesperson?

For me, speakers who have to read what they want to say are of no account. They simply have no credibility when it's obvious that they don't know their subject. They're unfamiliar with their own turf.

Notes never look good. Notes limit your body language. Notes kill your credibility. Next time you plan to wear earmuffs, think about using notes in public speaking, and put them in mothballs.

Release the delivery brakes and stop using notes.

THE GIGGLE

Michael from Barcelona — tall, olive skin, blue eyes, thick brown hair, handsome. Michael could portray a Malibu surfer in a sunscreen ad. He's the kind of guy who radiates charisma before he even opens his mouth.

But picture if you will, Michael's first speech in the seminar. He presented his life in three minutes. But right from the start we noticed something was wrong. He giggled — constantly.

I wasn't a good student — hehehehehe.

Oh, and I also have a girlfriend — hehehehehe.

I live in a beach town outside Barcelona — hehehehehe.

You can laugh on stage. You can make your audience laugh. You can tell a joke. But you cannot, you absolutely cannot giggle on stage.

Giggling expresses nervousness. Giggling drags down your authority. Giggling is more frequently a female phenomenon, but men do it too — like Michael. After four speeches and four rounds of feedback, Michael finally managed to lose the giggle. His authority finally lined up with his looks.

Release the delivery brakes and stop giggling.

AK-47

Do you know speakers who talk without a comma, period, or full stop?

Even if I'm a militant pacifist, I call these speakers AK-47s. They speak like an Avtomat-Kalashnikov 47 — rattattattattat.

You've already learned about the most effective word of all — the pause. AK-47 speakers don't pause at all — ever. Their pace is faster than Beep-Beep the Roadrunner. They don't give their audience any time to breathe, either. One of their speeches is like a never-ending climax.

The key word in "vocal variety" is *variety.* If you only speak rapidly, with high energy and pace, inevitably you will end up trapped in monotony as well.

I remember an evaluation Kim Page gave to my friend Melinda from Curaçao. Kim is an expert vocal coach, and Melinda was supposed to use vocal variety in her Toastmasters speech project.

Melinda talked about an experience she had with a huge hurricane during a stay in Puerto Rico. During her entire speech, Melinda was almost yelling.

In her evaluation, Kim paid tribute to the energy and authenticity Melinda had transmitted with the volume of her voice. But then she made a great observation while imitating Melinda's terrified voice from the Hurricane speech:

Melinda, your pacing, pitch and volume are great. But if you only use high pace, high pitch and high volume, it also becomes monotonous.

We all roared with laughter. Apart from the fact that the AK-47 speaking style quickly gets boring, it also prevents any suspense or drama from

developing. All the pauses get shot dead. So be a militant pacifist — turn
in your AK-47.

Release the delivery brakes, and don't speak like an AK-47.

DO YOU LIKE TO FEEL EXCLUDED?

Obviously, looking into the eyes of the people in your audience is a delivery
booster. But since the vast majority of speakers are much better at avoiding
eye contact than making it, I include this as a delivery brake.

Public speakers look everywhere — except into people's eyes. Some of
them look at the shoes of the people in the first row. There are visionary speakers — ones who only look at the back wall or out the windows
on the sides. There are contemplative speakers, who only look at a spot
on the floor in front of them. Once I even put a cross made of black
tape on the floor for a lawyer who only looked at that spot. I told him:
It's so you can focus on it better!

Then there are the psychopaths, who always look a few centimeters above
the heads of their audience.

Some speakers do look at people's eyes, but they only target subgroups. I
call them socialists if they only look at the left wing of their audience, and
conservatives if they only look at the right wing. And of course there are
centrists, too.

When I address the topic of eye contact in my seminars, I always talk to
two or three people on one side of the room. I keep looking at them while I
speak with another person sitting on the other side of the room.

*So how does it feel, Marly, when I talk about the art of rhetoric, and I only
look at Christian and Tony? How do you feel?*

Well, I feel excluded somehow.

So — you feel excluded. Do you like to feel exluded?

No!

Dear reader, do you like to feel excluded? No? Well, your audience doesn't either! To date I haven't met anyone who likes to feel excluded. But that's exactly what you do to people if you don't look them in the eyes. All of them, the entire audience. You cannot look two centimeters above their heads. You cannot look at their shoes. And the only time you're allowed to look at the back wall of the room is when you ask a visionary question: *Where do I see our company in five years from now?*

In all other cases, take conscious control of your eyes. Your eyes are a lighthouse. Left and right, right and left, left and right, covering the whole room. Direct eye contact, one person at a time, transmits self-confidence and authority. You're in charge. You rule the moment.

You're speaking to every single individual in the audience. Make sure no one feels excluded.

Release the delivery brakes; stop excluding people with your eyes.

WE WERE NOT BUILT IN 2,000 YEARS

Once I attended a workshop given by my friend Dr. Thomas Rose, a fantastic speaker and communications trainer from Cologne. Thomas asked us this question: *If your consciousness were one centimeter long, how long would your subconscious be?*

10 centimeters, 50 centimeters, one meter, even ten meters — the group offered quite a variety of answers.

Then Thomas gave us the real answer: *50 kilometers.*

It's our subconscious that tells us whether we like someone before they even begin to speak. It's our instincts reacting to their subconscious impressions that drive our opinions and decisions.

It's very clear that we weren't built in 2,000 years. We were built over millions of years. As a public speaker, you need to be aware of that!

When you see a speaker on stage with his hands in his pockets, your one centimeter tells you that it's a casual, informal pose. Maybe it's a little too casual, but still, it's just fine.

Your 50 kilometers tell you something completely different. What does your subconscious tell you? Have you ever thought about it?

Your subconsciousness tells you that the speaker is hiding something. It tells you there's danger! Of course, your conscious brain tells you that it's all fine, and that he's not hiding a weapon in his pockets. But — 50 kilometers is a lot bigger than one centimeter. Hidden hands cause distrust.

That's why I urge you: take your hands out of your pockets. Also, don't hide your hands behind your back. Don't even put your thumbs in your pockets.

Instead, build trust by showing your hands. Open your fingers; be transparent at all times. Transparency builds trust. And again, people won't know why they like you — they just will.

Release the delivery brakes and stop hiding your hands.

THE FORBIDDEN ZONE

A typical situation during a slide presentation: the presenter clicks to the next slide, which shows a graph, numbers, text, more text, more numbers, and a second graph. Then she turns to face the screen and continues to speak while showing her back to the audience. She walks over to the screen and, with her back facing the audience, she explains the number–graph–text salad.

If hiding your hands causes uneasiness in the cerebella of your audience, then showing your back is a declaration of war. In your hands you could hide a sharp object; behind your back you can hide a tank!

Your back is the forbidden zone. Nobody in your audience should ever be allowed to see it.

Sure, there are situations in which it is unavoidable, such as in the example above. What I recommend is that you stop talking, walk quickly over to the screen, position yourself at the side of the screen, and explain your slide information while your chest is facing your audience. Face front!

Why stop talking? Because your voice won't be projected at your audience. It will hit one of the walls, not their ears — although this isn't a problem if you're using a microphone. But this is all merely hypothetical, because you are not going to show your back to your audience!

Your back is the forbidden zone!

Release the delivery brakes: don't show your back to the audience.

TEAR DOWN THIS WALL

You can hide your hands. You can turn around and hide your entire body. And you can hide behind walls.

When Ronald Reagan told Mikhail Gorbachev to tear down the Berlin Wall, he had a good reason. The regime was hiding behind the wall, and the people couldn't be free. That wall had to be torn down — and so it happened.

People who speak in public try to hide behind walls all the time. It's not the Berlin Wall — it's lecterns, tables, and crossed, folded arms.

I say, tear down those walls!

All speakers who use notes, placing them on a lectern in front of them, are dead fish. They swim with the flow. Everybody does it.

Once I moderated a Rotarian event at Camp Nou, the football shrine of F.C. Barcelona. All the speakers used that stupid lectern. All but one used notes, but *all* of them stayed behind that column of plastic.

Why?

Don't be a dead fish! Step out from behind that lectern. You don't need it. Show your body; show your gestures; show your *self!*

Tables are another kind of wall. For a long time I preached the same old song, but I had no proof of the concept. I told everyone that, even if you participate in a roundtable discussion sitting behind tables, once it is your turn, you should grab a microphone, stand up, and speak up.

I told everyone, *Hey, I'd do it.* Then along came my friend Peter McKenzie from Citigroup. With a big fat smile he told me that he had finally done it. Picture a roundtable discussion, everybody seated — he stood up to speak and rocked the show. Only dead fish swim with the flow!

The third wall is more subtle. It's your arms crossed in front of your chest. In the US it's a signifier of power, but in the rest of the world it transmits distance, distance, distance.

Whether it's your arms, a table or a lectern — follow Ronald Reagan's advice to Gorbachev.

Release the delivery brakes and tear down those walls.

DON'T DO THE TWIST

In the Delivery Boosters section, you've already learned about the impact of hand gestures and holograms. If there is light, there is darkness, and where there are boosters, there are also brakes.

In my seminars I have identified the four usual suspects, four hand gestures that you'll absolutely avoid in the future.

HAND WASHING

Please wash your hands in the sink, not on stage.

PRAYING

Please pray in church, not on stage.

THE DIAMOND

Some call it a rhombus; some call it superglue (thanks to Angela Merkel). I call it the diamond: both hands touch at the fingertips and thumbs; the fingers point downward, the thumbs point up, creating a diamond shape. Whatever you call it, do please avoid this hand gesture. Here's a shocking confession — I used the diamond myself in the trailer for *The Seven Minute Star.*[10] Public speaking is a mountain without a peak — you can always climb higher.

WEDDING RING TWIST

This hand gesture is so hidden, so subtle — I could hardly find an image — but I did. Don't be twisting your wedding ring, or any other rings, when you speak. This hand gesture is good for only one thing — it reveals how nervous you are. But the weirdest thing is that some people do the twist with rings that aren't even there — phantom rings, missing rings.

Release the delivery brakes: don't use meaningless hand gestures.

CLAP, CLAP, OUCH

Another hand movement that's really annoying to audiences, despite its energetic nature, is clapping.

Every time you clap your hands, it makes a disturbing sound. It's even worse when you have a microphone clipped to your shirt or jacket that magnifies the clapping sound.

It's as simple as that: If you're in the audience, clap. If you're on stage, *don't.*

Release the delivery brakes and don't clap your hands.

---

10 www.bit.ly/t7mstrailer

THE SCRATCHAZ

They're everywhere. They're indestructible. They're ubiquitous. They're unstoppable. They're the "scratchaz" — the nose scratcha, the arm scratcha, the face scratcha, the shoulder scratcha, the ear scratcha, the neck scratcha.

The scratchaz are a mean breed of subconscious behavior. Victims of scratchaz attacks tend to forget all about them. Dr. Skinner of the Institute of Behavioral Science in Singapore[11] says, *Scratchaz cause some sort of amnesia. We investigated this subject for five years. None of the victims could recall a thing.*

While the victims don't remember anything, eyewitnesses of scratchaz attacks have reported on the extent of the devastation. Henry H. from Atlantic City saw them: *This poor man. They were all over him. They sucked all the self-confidence right out of this guy. It was horrible to watch.*

Maria K. from Hamburg adds, *They inflict angst on their victims. Someone has to stop them!*

In the vast majority of cases, scratchaz attacks occur during public speeches. The challenge with fighting back the scratchaz is that they are deeply rooted in our subconsciousness. According to Dr. Skinner the only effective vaccine is feedback.

When you witness an attack, tell the victim about it right away — before it's forgotten, the renowned scientist suggests.

Release the delivery brakes, and beware of the scratchaz.

---

11 All names and institutions in this chapter are factitious.

AEROBIC PENGUIN

This is the delivery brake that causes the heartiest laughter in my seminars — the aerobic penguin.

You too can meet this sporty fellow.

To do so, position yourself in front of a full body mirror. Hold both hands tight at your side. Now, keeping your elbows straight, move both arms up 45°, then let them both drop back. Repeat this exercise several times.

I present to you: the aerobic penguin!

More than half of my seminar participants perform this exercise. The aerobic penguin transmits indifference or resignation, both of which are subtle messages that you are absolutely forbidden to convey if you want to be trusted or have any authority on the stage. If you want to look silly, go ahead and do it.

You move people to action with conviction, with determination, with energy. You don't move anyone to action with indifference or resignation.

Apart from the subconscious message you convey by playing the aerobic penguin, this move also makes a disturbing sound; it's almost as annoying as clapping your hands.

These are two good reasons to leave the aerobic penguin at your gym.

Release the delivery brakes: stop doing aerobic exercises on stage.

FLASHMOB

Like your pauses, your hand gestures present a challenge on the delivery side to your perception of yourself.

When we speak in public, our brain constantly tells us things that actually aren't true: *This pause is too long; make it shorter. This hand movement is too excessive, cut it back.*

But what our brain tells us has nothing to do with what our audience perceives. For them, one second equals one second. For them, a two-second hand gesture lasts two seconds, not 10 minutes, as our brain tries to tell us.

This is the last pattern I added to this book: the flashmob.

It happened during the feedback round at a seminar I gave for one of my clients, a global hotel group. During his speech, Martin had referred to a man in the back of his car. He had looked over his right shoulder for an instant and had stretched out his arm and his hand to indicate the position of that man.

The problem was, he made the movement too rapidly. It was like a flashmob: fast in, and fast out.

You increase the impact of your gestures when you take your time.

Picture the scene: you're trying to get your check in a restaurant; you shyly raise your arm — again, and again — up and down, up and down. Does that sound familiar to you?

I used to do that. But thanks to public speaking, I learned not only to raise my arm, but my self-confidence, as well. Now I raise my arm and keep it raised like at school. I'm patient; I keep it up there until a waiter sees me. The process goes faster because I create more impact with a more decisive gesture.

Don't go in and out with your gestures, like a flashmob. Take your time; hold your position longer; be patient. The impact of your movements will be that much greater.

Release the delivery brakes and stop rushing with your gestures.

EVERY STEP YOU TAKE

Poise. According to Merriam-Webster, "poise" means:

1) A stably balanced state: equilibrium

2) Easy self-possessed assurance of manner: gracious tact in coping or handling; also: the pleasantly tranquil interaction between persons of poise.

You need to be poised, in a stable state of control and equilibrium, to transmit authority and credibility.

So far I've talked a lot about your arms and your hands. Another part of your body strongly affects your poise — your legs and your feet.

Every time you take your stance to speak on stage, your poise becomes an active player in the impression you'll make. Your audience focuses on your full body, on your entire presence. In public speaking, every word counts, and every step you take matters.

I never went beyond the driving range in golf, but I did manage to learn that your feet must be well-grounded, in parallel position, approximately 20 centimeters, or 8 inches, apart. The same applies to public speaking.

Yet, people are incredibly creative in avoiding this natural stance.

Here are some examples of leg and foot movements you will avoid in the future:

THE DRUMMER

Some speakers move the front of one foot up and down the way you do when you play the drums — that's why I call it "the drummer".

THE BALLET DANCER

It's a favorite foot movement among female speakers, but I've seen men do it too: the ballet dancer. They put their weight on one foot and do a sort of dance with the other — drawing circles on the floor with it, or positioning it in a 90° angle next to their planted foot.

THE FLAMINGO

Once I had an anonymous lawyer in my workshop. She scratched the left hollow of her knee with her right foot. She looked like a flamingo. Never, ever stand like a flamingo on stage!

Not everyone plays golf, but we can all picture that stance: feet parallel, flat on the ground, 20 centimeters (8 inches) apart. This is the only pose that transmits authority and credibility. A flamingo is pretty and pink, but it's hardly authoritative.

Release the delivery brakes and avoid moving your feet around when you're standing.

CHA CHA CHA

On stage you have two basic choices for moving.

First, you can move horizontally — from left to right, from right to left. This is the way you should move on stage. I've already talked about this.

The second option is to move vertically on stage, front to back, back to front.

Horizontal movements on stage always look good, but you should avoid vertical movement. I call it the "Cha, Cha, Cha".

One, two, three – cha, cha, cha – four, five – cha, cha, cha.

Vertical stage movement, forward and back, transmits three things: nervousness, nervousness, and nervousness. Vertical stage movement damages any impression of authoritativeness.

My recommendation for you: Keep dancing the cha cha cha in your Latin dance group. On stage, keep moving horizontally.

Release the delivery brakes and stop dancing the cha cha cha on stage.

NO NOISE PLEASE

Coins in your pocket, multiple silver bracelets, or extensive ear decoration — always keep in mind that coins and accessories make noise.

You cannot be making any extraneous noise when you're on stage; there should only be the sound of your voice. The most ridiculous example is a male speaker's playing with the coins in his pocket — it's a priceless "not to do".

Before you get up on stage to speak, make sure you replace dangling, jingling earrings with short earrings, get rid of bracelets and other distracting accessories, and take the coins and keys out of your pockets.

Release the delivery brakes: get rid of any disturbing noise.

DO YOU WANT TO FEEL DISRESPECTED?

The second most important moment of your speech is the last moment. In my experience, almost all public speakers screw up in those very last few seconds.

Just as your speech doesn't start with the first words you utter, your speech doesn't end with your last words, either. Your speech ends when you sit down — and not before.

Having given hundreds of seminars and seen thousands of speeches, I have witnessed only a handful of people who finished effectively. Most are simply overwhelmed — they feel overexposed. Hardly anyone can cope with the applause they receive. Almost all of them run away, like frightened chickens.

As soon as they've said their final words, and the applause starts to swell, they're gone. This is so uncool when you speak at any sort of event. The moderator is coming over to shake hands with you — but you've gone missing! The moderator even has to resort to chasing you down to shake hands with you. What a lousy final impress on!

The chair waiting back down there in the audience is like a black hole. The gravity of its attraction is irresistible. The audience's applause feels like a nuclear attack against the cerebellum. It yells: *Get outta here! Now!*

As I keep saying, our own perception is one thing, but the audience's perception is something else entirely. I always ask the same question in my seminars, after someone once again has run away like a frightened chicken. I approach another participant and ask: *So what did you feel when you were applauding Marc, and he ran away?*

After insisting, and repeating the same question a couple of times, I always unearth the same perception: *Well, I felt a bit disrespected.*

Exactly. This is what happens. With their applause, your audience is giving you a gift. By running away, you reject that gift — you disrespect your audience!

Do you like feeling disrespected? No? Do you want your audience to feel that you disrespect them?

Then here's how you'll do it in the future:

You say your last words. You take a half-step backwards. You shut up; you smile; and you stay still. When the applause starts to attack your cerebellum, push it back, stand still, and smile. After a while, about five seconds, you'll either stretch your hand out for the event moderator to grasp, or, absent one, you'll walk deliberately back to your chair and sit down. Only then you are allowed to say something about your performance. I don't want to hear any self-critical after-speech comments before you've sat down.

That's how to close!

Release the delivery brakes: don't be a chicken, and stop giving a negative final impression.

III. SLIDES

SLIDE BOOSTERS

PLUSPLUS PATTERNS THAT IMPROVE YOUR
PRESENTATIONS EVERY TIME YOU APPLY THEM

TWO VERSIONS

Think about all the slide presentations you've given so far in your life
— the monthly business reviews in front of the board, the sales presen-
taions at automotive congresses throughout the world, the strategic
plans for your department, the action plans for your franchise. Let your
mind travel, and go through all those slide presentations.

And let me ask you a simple question: How many presentations, how
many physical dot-ppt documents (in the case of PowerPoint), how
many individual files, did you prepare for each of these occasions?

In my first three years of giving public speaking trainings, only two
people said: *Two versions.*

Everyone else has told me they only had one version. Most people only
produce a single slide presentation for their talk — whatever event or
occasion they've created it for. But you'll do it differently from now on.

I differentiate between handout presentations and screen presentations.
Handout presentations are exactly what you did in the past: the slides
in your handouts would consist of all the text, statistics, charts, and
graphs needed to make your point when communicating with a reader.

You use handouts when you sit at a table with a couple of clients or
colleagues and discuss a particular issue by referring to those slides.

But for each time you present your slides on a screen, standing in front
of a group, from now on you'll create a second version — the screen
version of your presentation.

Based on your data-driven handouts, you create the screen presentation. Your screen presentation is driven by images, keywords, and key

numbers. The following chapters focus on screen presentations. You will learn about dos and donts, about boosters and brakes.

Boost your slides by creating a second version, just for your screen presentations.

KISS

Leonardo di ser Piero da Vinci was an Italian Renaissance polymath: painter, sculptor, architect, musician, scientist, mathematician, engineer, inventor, anatomist, geologist, cartographer, botanist, and writer. He is widely considered to be one of the greatest painters of all time, and he was perhaps the most diversely talented person who ever lived.[12]

One of my favorite quotations is: *Simplicity is the ultimate sophistication.* Leonardo da Vinci embodied and lived it.

Steve Jobs, whose principle of simplicity provides the key to your success with screen presentations, must have been a great fan of Da Vinci.

We often mention the KISS principle of public speaking, which is very much in line with Da Vinci and Jobs. KISS stands for: *Keep It Simple and Smart!*

Less is more for content; less is more for slides. Fewer colors, less text, fewer numbers, fewer logos — less, less, less.

When you create screen presentations, think of Leonardo Da Vinci and Steve Jobs. How would they do it? What would their design look like?

Boost your slides by keeping it simple and smart. KISS!

---

12 Wikipedia.org

BLACK OR WHITE

There's a Michael Jackson song that has the hookline: *It Don't Matter If You're Black Or White.* Do you remember?

Also remember, the same thing applies to your slide background colors. KISS — Keep it Simple and Smart. Any colors besides black or white interfere with both your text and your images.

Public speakers use an incredible potpourri of background colors — light green, dark orange, shining yellow, boring brown. Their standard excuse is that it was the template they used.

But you don't have to use a corporate template or any other template for your screen presentations. You're as free as a bird; you're not a dead fish. Did you ever see Steve Jobs do a screen presentation with an Apple, Inc., corporate template?

No, you didn't! He used dark blue tones.

You're always on the safe side with black and white. In all my seminars I take a mini-survey to find out people's preference about black and white. I write some text lines in black on a white background. A second slide shows the same lines in white letters on a black background.

Three quarters of the people, more or less, prefer the second version. Our brains can read white letters on a black background more easily. But I leave it to your personal taste; besides, you can use both styles in your presentation, if you want to.

But next time you choose your background colors for your slides, make sure you think of the King of Pop.

Boost your slides by limiting your background colors to black and white.

SIZE MATTERS

Another downside of handout presentations driven by corporate templates and thrown at the wall is the limitation of space. I've never understood why people don't use the whole screen. Whoever told you that you can't occupy the entire space of your slide?

A full screen image of a jungle looks so much more impressive than a small picture of a tree lost in a sea of white.

Or — Abraham Lincoln in six meters by four? Impressive!

Or the latest luxury car from Mercedes-Benz.

Only use high resolution for full-screen images — size matters! You can find them on numerous websites like Google or Bing, or specialized websites for royalty-free photos like Dreamstime.

This full-size requirement also applies to text.

Most of the search engine optimization presentations I've seen throw the keyword, *SEO*, up on the wall in Arial 20. It's much better to use large white letters, Calibri, font size 160, on a black background. That makes an impact!

As with background colors, people also are unsure of using the full screen. I hear it all the time:

No, we can't do this. We have to use our corporate templates!

Says who?

Our marketing department.

I see. And if you use another style in your screen presentation, would they drag you off the stage and beat you up in the alley?

I tell you, they won't. Slides are two-dimensional visual aids. Steve Jobs knew this very well. I never saw him use a single slide with the Apple logo in the upper right corner and a footer saying:

© 2011 Apple Inc. – Presentation iPhone 4 – Steve Jobs

I only saw wonderful large numbers, large buzzwords, large images expressing large visions.

There's more power in your point when you make a point of making it large. Don't settle for XS. Go for XXXL. In screen presentations, size does matter!

And the marketing department? Do it like Bismarck: send them a submission of indemnity once you've triumphed with your presentation.

Boost your slides by making full use of the screen.

MOMENT OF TRUTH

I told you before about the three moments of truth that boost your delivery at the very beginning of your speech: shut up, wait, and smile.

When you use slides, you'll want to take another moment of truth into consideration. When you use slides for your presentation, the first impression you make on your audience is not of you, but of your first slide.

Frequently your first slide is already up when you walk up the steps to the stage. This is a key moment, another moment of truth.

Let's stay with the *SEO* example. In accordance with the dictates of the marketing department, the dead fish presentation shows a standard first slide, which includes:

Name of the presenter

Title of the presenter

Name of the presenter's company

Logo of the presenter's company

Title of the speech

Location

Date

Maybe your first sentence will be different after reading this book, but your slide will still speak for you:

Hello, my name is XYZ. I'm ABC at DEF. Today I will talk about GHI. It's a great pleasure blah blah blah.

The core purpose of search engine optimization is to make sure that the client will have a top ranking on all major search engines. Thanks to SEO, the client's website stands out from the billions of other websites, with the result that internet users can easily find it.

I went looking for a metaphor and came up with the traditional image of the needle in a haystack.

Imagine a different first slide — one that doesn't show the standard information that bores the audience to death before the speaker even gets started.

Imagine instead a huge, five by four meter image, a close up of a yellow haystack with a silvery needle stuck into it.

Imagine how the speaker walks up on stage, takes a position in the center of the stage, right at the line of proximity. The speaker shuts up, waits, smiles. Then, with good volume, slow pace, and a well-placed pause, the presentation begins:

With us — your clients find that needle!

That's different. The audience awaits the beginning of the presentation with anticipation. One metaphorical image, full screen, expresses the core mission of the business better than a thousand words.

Don't waste this powerful moment of truth!

Boost your slides by showing a full screen metaphorical image as a first slide, transmitting your core message.

TWO RIVALS

Image and text — two eternal competitors fighting for preeminence on your slides.

When you make an image small, and add text next to it, you lose the visual impact of the image. That is not good!

When you use full screen images and put your text on top, the text drowns in the visual power of the image.

But — there's a trick.

I always use full screen images. Then I put a black text box on top of the image, adapting the size of the box to the length of the text. If you raise the transparency level of the text box by 20 to 30%, you'll see how both elements, image and text, manage to cooperate.

By using partially transparent text boxes on top of images, you pave the way for both of them to participate on your slides. And — it looks great!

Boost your slides by combining images with partially transparent text boxes.

ONE IS BETTER THAN TWO

Apart from floating along with the flow like a dead fish, there is an obvious reason people create handouts with detailed facts and figures, and then put them up on screen: they don't know their content. They need all the information they've put on the slides. Eventually, they simply read it out loud.

Using notes in public speaking is like wearing earmuffs — and that doesn't change when you hide behind sophisticated slides. The effect is the same: low ethos, low credibility, low persuasive power.

If you don't know your content, don't speak about it in public. If you need more preparation, take more time to prepare.

A 30-minute presentation featuring 15 slides is a challenge, I agree. But there's a smart way to guide yourself through your own content.

Full sentences are absolutely forbidden on screen. A typical sentence would be:

Our market share in 2012 has increased by 3%.

An audience that sees a full sentence automatically reads it, inevitably. An audience that's reading isn't listening to you. You want your audience to listen to you — from the first word till your very last syllable.

One smart way to deal with this is to reduce the sentences in your screen presentations to an absolute minimum, so your audience won't know in advance what you're going to tell them.

Take the sentence above. What's the most important information in the sentence?

Two options: market share, or 3%.

Personally I prefer the 3%. When you put "3%" up on the wall, the audience will hang on your words. They won't know what that's supposed to mean, so their curiosity will be stoked.

Now — what does it look like when you have a list of statements in your handout presentation?

Example:

Competition has become more intense in our core business segments due to three new Asian competitors.

New product launches exceeded expectations in both revenues and market penetration.

Our total market share in the last fiscal year has increased by 3%.

The corresponding screen presentation would say:

Competition

Products

3%

For you as the presenter these buzzwords and buzznumbers are great
— you know what you're going to say, but your audience doesn't. They
only have one option: they have to listen to you.

I'm a great fan of one-worders. Two words, like "New Products", are all
right, but going for three is pushing it — it's too close to being a sentence again. You can reduce any phrase to one or two words. Try it in
your next presentation.

Boost your slides by reducing words and numbers to the minimum.

ALPHANUMERIC MEETS GRAPHIC

When my seminars begin, I ask the participants to write down two of
their concrete expectations; then I ask them to select the most important one of those. And I say:

*Now, the alphanumerical guys among you, make a cross next to the most
important expectation you have for these two days. The graphical guys,
please, make a circle around your number one expectation.*

About half of your audience is alphanumeric, while the other half is
oriented more toward graphics. In your slides you can combine
alphanumeric and graphic elements; as a consequence, you appeal to
your entire your audience.

Example: The Top 5 Success Factors

In the Twitterverse we live in, it's all about Top 3, Top 5, Top 7, Top 10 lists. Sometimes I use lists like this in my screen presentations. But instead of using those horrid bullet points (I loathe and detest bullet points!), I prefer a climax-based alphanumeric-graphic combination. This one uses numbers, words, and graphic boxes:

1	PRODUCTS
2	PROCESSES
3	PEOPLE
4	CULTURE
5	CLIENTS

Boost your slides by combining text and numbers with graphic elements like boxes, triangles or circles.

THE POWER OF EQUATIONS

In the content booster chapter above, "Math Makes Marvelous Messages", you learned about the explanatory power of simple equations.

Like your math teacher in high school, you can show your equations — with large, larger, and even larger fonts.

A great side effect of slides with equations on them is that you can stay on that one slide for a longer time, and explain all the elements and their correlations. Few things are more annoying than someone rushing through 48 slides in seven minutes.

Boost your slides by presenting intriguing equations.

A.C.R.O.N.Y.M.S.

AIDA, B2B, BPO, BRIC, CPT, EBITDA, GAAP, IP, IPO, ISO, JIT, KPI, LIFO, MBA, NLP, ROI, PEST, SWOT, ...

Business presenters love to use acronyms both in their spoken and written language, but too often we assume that everyone in the audience knows what they mean. Acronyms make it too easy to fall into that trap of making general assumptions.

Once a friend who was on a working visit to Barcelona spent the day with me at my flat. She worked for Procter & Gamble, which is one of those companies that have an acronym fetish. I hardly understood half of what she was saying, it was so chock full of abbreviations and acronyms.

When you present in front of a group, always make sure to explain what your acronyms stand for.

Once you've done that, acromyms offer two great advantages for screen presentations:

Curiosity: An audience loves to be curious. When they read KISS or PEST or SPEAKER, they are intrigued right away. Curiosity keeps the tension level in the room high.

Memory: The reason acronyms exist is that they're easy to remember — or almost impossible to forget.

My friend, Professor Conor Neill of IESE Buiness School, always ends the theoretical part of his public speaking classes with the acronym SPEAKER:

S – Stories

P – Preparation

E – Energy

A – Authority

K – Knowledge

E – Experience

R – Reason

I haven't forgotten the SPEAKER acronym since the first time I saw it in Conor's class. Acronyms are very powerful when they're used effectively.

Boost your slides by including intriguing and memorable acronyms.

SPEAK AND CLICK

I was 10 years old when Mr Zwicker came to our house for the first time. My mother wanted me to learn to play a musical instrument. My father rejected the idea of piano lessons thanks to his own childhood trauma with them, so they agreed on the clarinet, a woodwind.

Mr Zwicker was my clarinet teacher. I well remember how he said: *Florian, before you touch the instrument, I want to tell you something important. So far, you've breathed through your lungs. From now on I want you to breathe through the holes in your belt.*

That day, it sounded strange to me, but it has become one of my most fundamental lessons — for playing the clarinet, for singing, and for public speaking. But Mr. Zwicker taught me much more. I learned a lot about notes and chords, rhythm, pauses, and anticipation — a form of syncopation.

In music, anticipation occurs when a note is played before the chord to which the note belongs, and then resolves when the anticipated chord is finally played.

Your screen presentations can benefit from the same effect. I call it "Speak & Click".

Every time you click to your next slide, make a short introductory comment like,

What does our strategy for the next three years look like? [click]

Or:

Quality in products and services is not the only factor driving success. What's more important is the people behind them. [click]

Speak & Click requires that you know your slides very well. But it's worth the time, because it exudes such a professional impression. Most other speakers do the opposite; they do "Click & Speak":

[click] Ah, oh yes, and then we have our three-year strategy.

[click] And of course, as you can see, our people are also important.

In music, anticipation is an element that creates suspense. Use the same technique in your presentations!

Boost your slides by using "Speak and Click".

INTERSTITIALS

Lars Sudmann is a former manager at Procter & Gamble. As I did, he turned his passion for good public speaking into a profession. One of his specialties is virtual communication.

I saw Lars giving a presentation at a conference in Basel. His views about how to execute conference and video calls much more energetically were eye-opening, but I particularly liked another aspect of his presentation.

He used interstitials — blank slides, colored black. After showing each slide for a moment, he moved on to a blank slide. This automatically drew the full attention of his audience to him, as if there were no slides at all.

But there's more! Several times he added some audio files to the blank slides. Music and tones came out of the blue — or black. I was deeply impressed by the surprising effect.

Interstitials are always great when you give longer presentations. You can use them, for instance, when you do interactive exercises between segments, or engage in short group work sessions. They get the audience's eyes off the screen and back onto you.

Boost your slides by including interstitials — blank and black.

THE EXTRA MILE

At the beginning of this group of slide boosters, I recommended that you create two versions of slide packs — one for the handouts, and another for the screen. Normally, you'll pass out the handout version to your audience — *after* your presentation, of course — because there is only one thing more certain than "Amen" at church: that people will start flipping through your pages once they hold them in their hot little hands.

You do not want anyone flipping through pages while you're speaking. You want them to be listening. Let them flip later.

But do you need to pass out handouts at all?

At least with larger audiences, for example at conferences or congresses, I recommend you spare yourself those three hours copying 3,500 pages for the 100 people expected to be in the audience.

I haven't kept one single conference folder — believe me, I looked. Event organizers stuff 30 presentations into folders and expect you to put them next to the 37 other folders you collected at all those other conferences. Fortunately, USB has taken over.

Digital or paper — there is something much better that you can prepare.

When I worked as a business developer for KPMG in Spain, we had the idea to create one-page handouts for every important client meeting. A one-pager was the graphic-alphanumeric summary of the presentation handout.

In our one-pagers, we showed key points, key processes, key correlations, opportunities and threats, cost drivers, and other factors that would influence business performance.

I printed these one-pagers on a half page, and on the flipside I put our logo, contact info, and a hotline number. It was still a piece of paper. But then came the stroke of genius — I laminated it!

People throw away paper, but it's hard for them to throw away a laminated executive summary that looks more like a product or a souvenir.

You can do the same when you have important screen presentations. Forget about those 35 to 60 page behemoths; nobody wants to carry them home in the first place, and they'll certainly never read them again. Your time, effort, and money will probably end up in the trash bin at the car-park, the train station, or the airport.

Go the extra mile and use laminated one-pagers. They'll love them — and they'll *keep* them.

Boost your slides by preparing laminated one-page summaries as handouts for your audience.

SLIDE BRAKES

PLUSPLUS PATTERNS THAT IMPROVE YOUR PRESENTATIONS EVERY TIME YOU AVOID THEM

DON'T PAY THE PRICE

On any football pitch, there's one place you never go: you don't run into the goalkeeper! You keep clear, because if you don't, you *will* pay a price.

The beam of your slide projector is just the same — stay away from it, or you'll pay a price.

Every time you stand between the projector and the wall, you make a negative, unprofessional impression. You throw a shadow on the wall, your head shines like a Baroque statue of Mary Magdalene, you look like the proverbial deer caught in the headlights — it looks awful.

The rule is: don't get caught in that beam of light!

If you've read John Zimmer's checklist, as I've recommended that you do, you know that public speaking is all about preparation.

Even before you step in front of your audience, you'll know where the beam is. You'll know exactly where you can move on the stage without getting caught in the beam. There are no excuses in public speaking; there's only poor preparation.

Sometimes the projector gets put on a table in the middle of the room, so you have to stay to the left or right of the beam. Sometimes the projector hangs from the wall or the ceiling, so you can't move backwards or the shadow of your head will interfere with your slide.

Arrive early at the venue and check the stage setting. Following the advice of the abovementioned stage specialist Jerzy Zientkowski, on bigger stages I use tape to mark my performing territory. As I said, there are no excuses in public speaking!

Release the slide brakes and don't pay the price of getting caught in the beam.

ONE SLIDE, ONE MESSAGE

There's a saying: If your speech has two messages, give two speeches.

The same applies to your slides. People try to stuff too much information onto one slide. The source of this problem, of course, is that they are creating only a handout presentation.

I remember a sample slide that showed:

A product/cost/relationship triangle;

four questions about why, how and from whom the client buys, and who decides;

four business units classified according to their role in the process of creating value; and

a six-letter acronym showing all the personnel involved in the client's purchasing process.

TMI! Too Much Information! My alternative slide kept the triangle in the center, left out the questions (to be stated orally), and distributed the four business units in boxes (each containing identifiers of no more than two words) around the triangle. This used the full screen, with a black background. I put the acronym on a second slide.

Keep Your Screen Slides Simple and Smart — KYSSSS! No one limits the number of your slides. With 10 fully packed slides, you can talk for an hour. With 20 KYSSSS screen slides, you can speak for 10 minutes. It takes some practice, but you'll soon get a feeling for the timing.

If you follow the rule — one slide, one message — you'll be just fine.

Release the slide brakes and stop overloading your slides.

BULLETS OVERBOARD

What do you feel when you hear the word "dentist"? What do you feel when you remember the screeching sound of fingernails on a blackboard? What do you feel when you think of Oktoberfest without beer?

There are things in life that we just never want to think about: going to the dentist, the screeching sound of fingernails on a blackboard, Oktoberfest without beer — and bullet points on slides.

In the world of business presentations, there is an inexplicable paradox: everyone seems to agree with and support the idea of refraining from using bullet points on slides. And yet, everyone does it anyway!

Again, it's the handout vs. screen dilemma. Bullet points are fine on handout presentations. It's like in Word or other text programs — bullet points are so normal.

However, in screen presentations, they simply are not cool at all! Throw them overboard, kick them out, just get rid of them.

If you use one-worders or two-worders, as I described above, and if you put the words in boxes on top of full-screen images, also as I described above, all your bullets are history. That's an easy win.

You can leave the bullet points in your handout presentations. But every time you put things up on screen, think about dentists, screeching fingernails, and Oktoberfest without beer. No bullet points in screen presentations — Never!

Release the slide brakes and eliminate all bullets from your points.

IT'S NOT ABOUT YOU

In German we say: *Eigenlob stinkt.* Self-praise stinks. And dead fish certainly stink too.

Take a look at the slide presentations you see at conferences, in sales meetings, even in internal meetings — self-praise everywhere!

I'm talking about those corporate logos!

In 99% of all business presentations, I see the speaker's company logo either in the bottom-left or bottom-right corner. 35 times on 35 slides!

Hasn't it ever occurred to these people that they are the only ones who are all psyched up about their company logo?

Why should those 600 people in your audience care about your corporate logo?

You have it there because it's the corporate template, imposed by the marketing department. Have you ever thought about it? Marketing people, other than in the consumer goods industry, almost never speak with clients.

Marketing people don't talk to clients; sales people do!

And what do great sales people do? They ask questions — and what's more, they listen to the answers. Great sales people know we have two ears and one mouth. Great sales people know who the most important character is. It's the client.

So what are you doing? You're putting your logo up there — 35 times. Using your logo like that implicitly says, *I'm important. I'm a great brand. I have a great logo!*

And you know what? Your clients — your target group, your audience —could not care less.

I don't remember Steve Jobs presenting the iPhone with an Apple logo on the bottom-right corner of his slides.

Your logo belongs on handout presentations, but on screen presentations, you don't need to display your logo at all. It's not about you; it's about the audience!

Release the slide brakes and get rid of your logo.

A REGULAR DISASTER

Flying letters and phrases, dissolving boxes and circles, images popping up and disappearing; animations in screen presentations are a great tool if you want to distract and disturb both yourself and your audience.

Of all speakers I've seen using animation-filled presentations, almost nobody went through the talk 100% smoothly. A regular disaster happens when speakers use animated bullet point lists:

The first phrase appears and they read it out loud. Then they click and the second phrase appears, which they also read out loud. The same thing happens with the third and fourth phrases; they read them out loud too. They think they've reached the end of the list, and they concentrate on the next slide, which, wonder of wonders, they even remember. They use the trick of anticipation, and make an introductory statement. They click enthusiastically to the next slide and — OOPS — the fifth bullet point appears. They'd forgotten about that one. It's a regular disaster.

I cannot repeat it often enough: Screen animations distract and disturb both the speaker and the audience.

How could you handle the 5-point list from above in a smoother way?

Put five boxes on the slide — three in the lower row, two above — like the Olympic rings, centered upside down. Then put one word in each box. The audience cannot help listening to you, and you won't forget that fifth point. You won't accidentally repeat yourself, either. It's much smoother!

If you plan to build up the blocks one by one, to increase the suspense, I recommend you create five individual slides. It has the same effect on the audience, but you can print out your slides the way you present them. Animations and printing don't like each other very much.

You don't need animations at all. The slide boosters I've presented here — full-screen images, black backgrounds — have a much greater impact.

Release the slide brakes and avoid animations.

DON'T CONTACT US

Slides speak for themselves more than we think. For example, showing your logo on 35 slides is a not very subtle form of egocentrism.

But the climax of egocentricity comes with the standard next-to-last slide of literally all business presentations: it's the "Contact Us" slide.

Most of the time this slide says something like:

Contact us at info@abcdef.com or +1 111 111 111.

If you're a dead fish floating with the flow, then just keep including this standard egocentric slide. If, instead, you're alive, then do it better.

Jack Vincent, author of the sales bible *Snap, Crackle 'n' Pop,* and my personal sales guru, confirms that a pitch is never a presentation to sell. Its purpose is to start up a relationship with a prospective client.

Let's assume you're going to give a pitch presentation at a sector event to 150 potential buyers. You've explained the three top product characteristics and the three corresponding benefits. You've established a connection with your audience using all the PLUSPLUS patterns from this book. You've come to the next-to-last slide of your pitch presentation. It says: *"Contact us."* You're asking your prospects to contact you.

I don't know about your idea of service, but shouldn't it be *you* who's going to contact *them?* Wouldn't it convey a message of commitment and respect on your side?

I propose that you make your "Contact us" slide walk the plank. Instead, you could, for example, show a full-screen image of a cup of coffee, and say:

For the next step, I propose we have a coffee together here at this event — today or tomorrow — and I'll give you more information that's tailored to your situation.

When prospects are really interested, a statement like this makes sure that they feel appreciated. They don't have to contact you via email — they get an exclusive one-to-one meeting, and a free coffee!

It can be a cup of coffee, it can be a glass of beer, it can be the offer to call everyone who leaves a business card with you — but make sure you get rid of this egocentric slide, "Contact Us".

Release the slide brakes and throw out the "Contact Us" slide.

THE MOST BORING SLIDE

Just like the first moment of your presentation, the final impression you leave behind does not arise from your spoken words alone. You also leave a lasting impression with your last slide.

In my public speaking seminars, it usually takes the entire first day to catch all those "Thank-yous" at the end of speeches, and send them off for life to rhetoric prison.

On day two, the participants have to give a presentation with slides. The dilemma they face is that they are obligated to send me those slides a week before the seminar. Thus, when they make their presentation on day two, they have to combine dead fish slides with all the things they've learned on day one. That *is* a challenge.

The most laughter in the group always comes when the speakers click to their last slide, which almost always states,

Thank you for your attention!

Or:

Thank you very much!

In the "Content Boosters" section, you learned about how to raise goosebumps with your last sentence. You also learned that you could kill those goosebumps with just two words: *"Thank you"*.

Now — it helps nothing if you perfect your final spoken words, but show *"Thank you"* on your last slide.

That would be the most boring slide you'd have, because it's the most boring slide imaginable. Even a black interstitial slide is more interesting!

What I suggest is that you use the same slide at the end of your presentation that you did at the beginning. That is, the first slide is also the last. Apart from the more intriguing and inspirational visual effect, you reinforce the drainpipe — you bring your presentation full circle and leave the audience with a feeling of completion.

Release the slide brakes and don't say "Thank You" on your last slide.

PLUSPLUS IS MAGIC!

You've swum in the PLUSPLUS river with me. You decided to swim against the flow, instead of floating like a dead fish. Just like Sonia, you've reached the other side, where there are no rules or limitations; there are only creativity and inspiration.

Enjoy your new life on stage!

THE PLUSPLUS PATTERN LIST

In the list below you find a summary of all 108 PLUSPLUS patterns for better communication.

For each of your future speeches and presentations I suggest that you select three PLUSPLUS patterns and focus on them. Use a pencil to mark the corresponding numbers.

Less is more – always focus on three!

CONTENT BRAKES

ABOUT THE AUTHOR

Since Florian Mueck joined a chapter of Toastmasters International in Barcelona in 2005, public speaking has become his greatest passion. In 2009 the former business consultant turned his passion into a profession.

Today, a collaborator with IESE Business School in Barcelona and author of *The Seven Minute Star – Become a Great Speaker in 15 Simple Steps,* Florian offers communication seminars, presentation coaching, keynote speeches, and moderation in English, German, and Spanish — mainly to international corporations.

In 2012 Florian and John Zimmer, a fellow public speaking professional, introduced *Rhetoric — The Public Speaking Game™.*

For more information about Florian, visit:

www.florianmueck.com

Made in the USA
Charleston, SC
24 July 2014